Following Christ... The Man of God

A STUDY OF JOHN 6–14

BIBLE STUDY GUIDE

From the Bible-teaching ministry of

Charles R. Swindoll

INSIGHT FOR LIVING

Charles R. Swindoll is a graduate of Dallas Theological Seminary and has served in pastorates for more than twenty-four years, including churches in Texas, New England, and California. Since 1971 he has served as senior pastor of the First Evangelical Free Church of Fullerton, California. Chuck's radio program, "Insight for Living," began in 1979. In addition to his church and radio ministries, Chuck has written twenty-three books and numerous booklets on a variety of subjects.

Based on the outlines of Chuck's sermons, the study guide text is coauthored by Ken Gire, a graduate of Texas Christian University and Dallas Theological Seminary. The Living Insights are written by Bill Butterworth, a graduate of Florida Bible College, Dallas Theological Seminary, and Florida Atlantic University. Ken Gire is presently the director of educational products at Insight for Living, and Bill Butterworth is currently the director of counseling ministries.

Editor in Chief:	Cynthia Swindoll
Coauthor of Text:	Ken Gire
Author of Living Insights:	Bill Butterworth
Assistant Editor:	Karene Wells
Copy Manager:	Jac La Tour
Senior Copy Editor:	Jane Gillis
Copy Editors:	Kevin Moritz and Glenda Schlahta
Director, Communications Division:	Carla Beck
Project Manager:	Nina Paris
Project Supervisor:	Cassandra Clark
Art Director:	Donna Mayo
Production Artist:	Diana Vasquez
Typographer:	Bob Haskins
Calligrapher:	David Acquistapace
Cover:	Painting by Carl Bloch, *The Sermon on the Mount*
Print Production Manager:	Deedee Snyder
Printer:	Frye and Smith

ISBN 0-8499-8296-0

Ordering Information

An album that contains fourteen messages on seven cassettes and corresponds to this study guide may be purchased through the Sales Department of Insight for Living, Post Office Box 4444, Fullerton, California 92634. For ordering information and a current catalog, please write our office or call (714) 870-9161.

Canadian residents may obtain a catalog and ordering information through Insight for Living Ministries, Post Office Box 2510, Vancouver, British Columbia, Canada V6B 3W7, (604) 272-5811. Australian residents should direct their correspondence to Insight for Living Ministries, General Post Office Box 2823 EE, Melbourne, Victoria 3001. Other overseas residents should direct their correspondence to our Fullerton office.

If you wish to order by Visa or MasterCard, you are welcome to use our toll-free number, (800) 772-8888, Monday through Friday, between the hours of 8:30 A.M. and 4:00 P.M., Pacific time. This number may be used anywhere in the United States except Alaska, California, and Hawaii. Orders from these areas can be made by calling our general office number, (714) 870-9161. Orders from Canada can be made by calling (604) 272-5811.

Table of Contents

Following Christ . . . The Man of God
A Study of John 6–14

*The center section of John's Gospel allows us to walk
with Christ through numerous scenes. He faces criticism,
defends a helpless woman, gives sight to the blind, teaches
His disciples, raises the dead, and models humility by washing the feet of His closest friends. No one who closely follows someone that godly can remain the same.*

*Travel with me through these events. Use your imagina-
tion. Think of yourself as being a part of each scene. Don't
miss one detail. You will find that such godly qualities are
contagious. So be forewarned! Your life will begin to change.*

*As we study Christ's life, let's be careful not to limit our
thoughts or to concentrate our attention only on the printed
page. These are living truths designed to get inside our
lives. Let's allow them entrance.*

Chuck Swindoll

Putting Truth into Action

Knowledge apart from application falls short of God's desire for His children. Knowledge must result in change and growth. Consequently, we have constructed this Bible study guide with these purposes in mind: (1) to stimulate discovery, (2) to increase understanding, and (3) to encourage application.

At the end of each lesson is a section called 🌳 *Living Insights.* There you'll be given assistance in further Bible study, and you'll be encouraged to contemplate and apply the things you've learned. This is the place where the lesson is fitted with shoe leather for your walk through the varied experiences of life.

It's our hope that you'll discover numerous ways to use this tool. Some useful avenues we suggest are personal meditation, joint discovery, and discussion with your spouse, family, work associates, friends, or neighbors. The study guide is also practical for Sunday school classes, Bible study groups, and, of course, as a study aid for the "Insight for Living" radio broadcast.

In order to derive the greatest benefit from this process, we suggest that you record your responses to the lessons in the space which has been provided for you. In view of the kinds of questions asked, your study guide may become a journal filled with your many discoveries and commitments. We anticipate that you will find yourself returning to it periodically for review and encouragement.

Ken Gire
Coauthor of Text

Bill Butterworth
Author of Living Insights

Following Christ...
The Man of God

A STUDY OF JOHN 6–14

God's Specialty: Impossibilities
John 6:1–21

Impossibilities. Everyone can list a few. You can't make a silk purse out of a sow's ear. You can't get blood out of a turnip. You can't make a crab walk straight.

Yet Jesus knit His apostolic purse out of the frayed threads of local fishermen and tax gatherers; He got wine out of ordinary tap water; and He made a man, thirty-eight years lame, to walk. Impossible? The word wasn't even in Christ's vocabulary.

How about your vocabulary? Do words like *can't...won't work...impossible* leap from your lips? Has your pessimistic outlook imprinted these words in your mind? What's on your list of impossibilities? Your marriage, your job, your finances?

In today's lesson, we're going to see Jesus perform another impressive, seemingly impossible feat—the feeding of the five thousand. And if He can do that with only a few fish and loaves, imagine what He can do with your life and your impossibilities!

I. A Question of Perspective
The whole issue of impossibility is really one of perspective. To a child, many things seem impossible, like baking or long division. But from an adult vantage point, these things are not only possible, but can be handled with relative ease. Let's try to understand the impossible by looking at it from two different viewpoints, the human and the divine.

   A. The human perspective. Webster defines *impossible* as "incapable of being or of occurring ... insuperably difficult ... hopeless."[1] And so seem many of our circumstances when viewed horizontally.

   B. The divine perspective. From the vertical perspective, however, nothing is too heavy to lift when God holds the lever. The prophet Jeremiah makes that claim in his Old Testament book.

---

1. New Collegiate Dictionary, see "impossible."

1

" 'Ah Lord God! Behold, Thou hast made the heavens
and the earth by Thy great power and by Thine out-
stretched arm! Nothing is too difficult for Thee.' "
(Jer. 32:17)
God confirms Jeremiah's words later in the chapter.
"Behold, I am the Lord, the God of all flesh; is anything
too difficult for Me?" (v. 27)
And with resounding clarity, the New Testament echoes this
promise.
"For nothing will be impossible with God." (Luke 1:37)
"The things impossible with men are possible with
God." (18:27)
Two threads of truth run through both testaments. One, God's
power is unlimited. Two, God's promise is unconditional. Noth-
ing stands in His way—ever!

II. A Biblical Example

In John 6:1–15, the seemingly immovable object of human impossibility meets the irresistible force of divine power.

A. The setting. Verses 1–4 paint a backdrop for our scene.
After these things Jesus went away to the other side
of the Sea of Galilee (or Tiberias). And a great multitude was following Him, because they were seeing
the signs which He was performing on those who
were sick. And Jesus went up on the mountain, and
there He sat with His disciples. Now the Passover, the
feast of the Jews, was at hand.
Thousands of people have gathered in the area to celebrate the
Passover, and after preaching to them all day, Jesus and the
disciples desperately need rest and relaxation. But like Mardi
Gras throngs, the crowds press in, hoping to rub shoulders with
Jesus . . . and their needs take priority over any planned respite.

B. The opportunity. Great opportunities are often disguised as
unsolvable problems. The disciples try to get away, but a crowd
of curiosity-seekers takes precedence. Let's watch as a humanly
unsolvable problem becomes a great opportunity when seen
from a divine viewpoint.

1. **From a human perspective.** With their limited, human
understanding, these weary fishermen can see only a swell-
ing sea of humanity threatening to wash over them. In verse 10
we are told that this great multitude numbered five thousand
men. Including women and children, this figure could have
easily been eight or ten thousand.

2. **From a divine perspective.** From Jesus' point of view, the
crowds weren't an infringement but an opportunity . . . a

2

chance to reveal His glory and, at the same time, stretch his disciples' faith. He begins with a test for Philip.

"Where are we to buy bread, that these may eat?" (v. 5b)

Jesus' intent is not to humiliate or demean Philip; rather, He wants to stretch Philip's muscle of faith, to help him grow and make him stronger.

A Strategy for Stretching Faith

Philip's test is explained by the words "for He Himself knew what He was intending to do" (v. 6b), clearly indicating that Jesus is not only in control of the immediate circumstances but several steps ahead of the game.

Like a brilliant chess player, who thinks several moves ahead, Jesus plots a strategy to build the faith of His disciples. A chess player may give up a minor piece as a gambit in order to later gain an advantage, and so this King is willing to give up a little R and R for His troops in order to gain a more committed band of men.

When you realize that your circumstances, no matter how overwhelming or pressing, are ruled by a King who seeks your highest good, you can truly "consider it all joy . . . when you encounter various trials, knowing that the testing of your faith produces endurance . . . that you may be perfect and complete, lacking in nothing" (James 1:2–4).

Is that how you view circumstances that crowd you or bring unexpected pressure? If not, perhaps you need to square your circumstances on God's chessboard. Maybe then it will be easier to see His hand at work . . . and His strategy for stretching your faith.

C. The test. Actually, two disciples take the test this day. Philip is appointed—Andrew volunteers.

  1. **Philip.** With computer speed, Philip analyzes the situation and gives Jesus a spread-sheet answer.

"Two hundred denarii worth of bread is not sufficient for them, for everyone to receive a little." (John 6:7)

A denarius was approximately a day's wages for the common laborer (Matt. 20:2). Philip is quick to come to the bottom line in terms of dollars and cents—dollars and cents

3

they don't have, he implies. However, Philip's balance sheet doesn't show the infinite wealth and power of God, who owns the earth and all it contains (Ps. 24:1) and who can do "exceeding abundantly beyond all that we ask or think" (Eph. 3:20). So how does Philip do on his exam? Not so well. He fails in three areas. One, he sees only the situation—not the solution. Two, he's more concerned about the odds against them than about those for them. Three, he calculates for only a bare minimum—"for everyone to receive a little."

2. **Andrew.** While Philip busily burns out the batteries in his pocket calculator, Andrew scurries among the crowd looking for groceries.

> One of His disciples, Andrew, Simon Peter's brother, said to Him, "There is a lad here who has five barley loaves and two fish, but what are these for so many people?" (John 6:8–9)

Andrew, who has volunteered for this test, scores somewhat better than Philip. A careful optimist, Andrew at least seeks a solution, even though it is a human one. Putting his nose in a kid's picnic basket, he finds five flat barley loaves and a couple of pickled sardines.[2] Admittedly, it isn't much, but Andrew's approach is better than Philip's. However, he also becomes overwhelmed by the circumstances: "but what are these for so many people?"

Looking for Loaves in All the Wrong Places!

Philip sees the impossible circumstances surrounding them and looks first at the budget. Andrew sees the same circumstances and checks the pantry.

But neither of them thinks to look to the Lord. Seems strange, doesn't it? Particularly after they have seen Him change water into wine.

But then, don't we respond in much the same way. We've all seen Jesus work miracles in our lives. We've seen Him change the old water of our lives into new wine. We've seen Him give new legs of faith to our lame spiritual bodies. Yet when faced with impossible circumstances, how soon we forget the power of our God.

The next time you're faced with the impossible, try not to look at your bank account or at your Old Mother

---

2. "Barley bread was bread of a cheap kind, so that the boy was probably poor. The two fishes were something of a [tidbit] which would make the coarse barley bread more palatable." Leon Morris, *The Gospel According to John* (Grand Rapids, Mich.: William B. Eerdmans Publishing Co., 1971), p. 344.

4

Hubbard cupboards. Look first to Jesus, the bread of
life, who can do "exceeding abundantly beyond all
that we ask or think."

D. The response.

1. **Jesus'.** Verses 10–13 record Jesus' miraculous response to
the impossible.

> Jesus said, "Have the people sit down." Now there
> was much grass in the place. So the men sat down,
> in number about five thousand. Jesus therefore
> took the loaves; and having given thanks, He dis-
> tributed to those who were seated; likewise also
> of the fish as much as they wanted. And when
> they were filled, He said to His disciples, "Gather
> up the leftover fragments that nothing may be
> lost." And so they gathered them up, and filled
> twelve baskets with fragments from the five bar-
> ley loaves, which were left over by those who
> had eaten.

Calmly and methodically, Jesus sits the people down, divid-
ing them into manageable groups of hundreds and fifties
(see Mark 6:40). And taking the scant supply of groceries,
He looks to God in prayer and multiplies the food for the
masses. Not only does the lad's lunch box give everyone "a
little" (John 6:7), it is enough in the hands of the Lord to
give everyone "as much as they wanted" (v. 11). And not
only that, there are twelve baskets full of leftovers—one for
each of the disciples! Philip and Andrew are probably
scratching their heads in amazement, while a poor kid with
a Cheshire grin is putting his thumbs in his suspenders and
rocking back on his heels.

2. **The disciples'.** After feeding the five thousand, Jesus throws
a pop quiz at the disciples. Mark 6:45–51 expands on this
incident and provides us with the disciples' embarrassing
scores.

> And immediately He made His disciples get into
> the boat and go ahead of Him to the other side
> to Bethsaida, while He Himself was sending the
> multitude away. And after bidding them farewell,
> He departed to the mountain to pray. And when
> it was evening, the boat was in the midst of the
> sea, and He was alone on the land. And seeing
> them straining at the oars, for the wind was
> against them, at about the fourth watch of the

night, He came to them, walking on the sea; and He intended to pass by them. But when they saw Him walking on the sea, they supposed that it was a ghost, and cried out; for they all saw Him and were frightened. But immediately He spoke with them and said to them, "Take courage; it is I, do not be afraid." And He got into the boat with them, and the wind stopped; and they were greatly astonished.

The next verse reads like a note in a teacher's grade book.

For they had not gained any insight from the incident of the loaves, but their heart was hardened. (v. 52)

3. **The people's.** Turning back to John 6, we see the response of the people.

When therefore the people saw the sign which He had performed, they said, "This is of a truth the Prophet who is to come into the world." Jesus therefore perceiving that they were intending to come and take Him by force, to make Him king, withdrew again to the mountain by Himself alone. (vv. 14–15)

They see the miracle, and the gears in their minds begin to turn in selfish and manipulative circles. Jesus is indeed King of the Jews, but when He does reign, it will be on His terms, not on man's or Satan's (Matt. 4:8–10, John 6:15).

4. **Yours.** Having seen this miracle of Christ, how will you respond? Like Philip, with pessimism? Like Andrew, with guarded optimism? Like the other disciples, who seem to have slept through the whole lesson? Or like the eager young boy, excited to give what little he has and watch with wide eyes how the Lord will use it to overcome the impossible!

Living Insights

Study One ■■■

To get an overview of the passages we'll cover in this study guide, read through the middle portion of John's Gospel. This will help you know where you're going before you begin the journey.

• Take your time and carefully read John 6–14. As you do, you will undoubtedly be struck with certain thoughts, questions, and general observations. Record one general observation for each chapter in the chart on the following page.

6

Following Christ . . . The Man of God	
Chapter	Observation
6	
7	
8	
9	
10	
11	
12	
13	
14	

Continued on next page

🌹 *Living Insights*

From time to time we are all faced with great opportunities brilliantly disguised as unsolvable problems. What is the great opportunity in your life right now? Do you have the proper perspective on this impossible situation? What part does God play in this difficult time? Reflect on God's specialty by jotting down your thoughts on the following questions.

● What is your impossibility?

● How long have you been enduring this situation?

● Why can't human solutions help?

● Where is God in this circumstance?

● Looking at your impossible situation from God's perspective, can you map out the right direction for your life?

Bread Delivered from Heaven
John 6:22-71

During 1789-1815, France was in the throes of a tumultuous revolution. It was a time when wealthy aristocrats traveled in extravagant carriages while ragged paupers begged on the streets. For the aristocrat, life was a smorgasbord; for the destitute, a soup line.

Revolutionary France parallels the way many of us live our lives. Indulgence and indigence live side by side within our borders. We have the outward appearance of aristocracy, but inside we are poverty-stricken. We wine and dine at the finest of restaurants, while inside our spirits slowly starve.

Just as there is a physical hunger that only physical food can satisfy, so there is a deeper, spiritual hunger in the pit of man's soul that only spiritual food can nourish.

In today's lesson Jesus tells us to work not "for the food which perishes, but for the food which endures to eternal life" (John 6:27a). In doing so, He echoes the advice of Isaiah: "Why do you spend money for what is not bread, / And your wages for what does not satisfy?" (Isaiah 55:2a).

I. Preliminary Events

The feeding of the five thousand in the first part of John 6 was the lab in which Jesus demonstrated His power over creation. In the remainder of the chapter, Jesus now takes the lab lessons and organizes them into a profound lecture that many commentators call the Bread of Life Discourse. Perhaps for the first time, the crowd that was fed the bread and fish dinner actually had all they wanted to eat (see vv. 11b–12a). It is no wonder, then, that the crowd intently followed this miracle worker. After all, where else could they find an abundance of food? Consequently, when the next day came and their hunger returned, they looked for Jesus (vv. 22–25).

II. Preeminent Issues

The miraculous feeding of the five thousand raises some important issues.

A. Clarification of motives. First and foremost is the crowd's motive for seeking Him, which Jesus addresses in verses 26–27. "Truly, truly, I say to you, you seek Me, not because you saw signs, but because you ate of the loaves, and were filled. Do not work for the food which perishes, but for the food which endures to eternal life, which the Son of Man shall give to you, for on Him the Father, even God, has set His seal."[1]

Notice the contrast drawn in verse 27 between "food which perishes" and "food which endures," reminiscent of His words to the woman at the well (4:13–14). There are two kinds of hunger and two kinds of food—physical and spiritual. Jesus' point is that all these people are interested in is physical satisfaction—they're more interested in their stomachs than in their hearts, more intent on the here and now than on the hereafter.

Evaluating Your Motives

Jesus tells us in the Sermon on the Mount: "Do not be anxious for your life, as to what you shall eat, or what you shall drink; nor for your body, as to what you shall put on. Is not life more than food, and the body than clothing?" (Matt. 6:25).

Take a moment to examine your anxieties. Do you work for "food which endures," or is getting your daily bread your all-consuming passion? Jesus goes on to offer guidance for getting out of the valley of worry.

"Do not be anxious then, saying, 'What shall we eat?' or 'What shall we drink?' or 'With what shall we clothe ourselves?' For all these things the Gentiles eagerly seek; for your heavenly Father knows that you need all these things. But seek first His kingdom and His righteousness; and all these things shall be added to you." (vv. 31–33)

B. Discussion of miracles. Their mistaken motives brought to light, the crowd responds with a question that exposes their need for instruction.

"What shall we do, that we may work the works of God?" Jesus answered and said to them, "This is the work of God, that you believe in Him whom He has sent." (vv. 28–29)

---

1. Commenting on the latter part of verse 27, William Barclay notes: "It was not the *signature*, but the *seal* that authenticated. In commercial and political documents it was the seal, imprinted with the signet ring, which made the document valid; it was the seal which authenticated a will; it was the seal on the mouth of a sack or a crate that guaranteed the contents." With each miracle performed, God's authenticating seal on Christ's life was evident to all. William Barclay, *The Gospel of John,* vol. 1, rev. ed., The Daily Study Bible Series (Edinburgh, Scotland: Saint Andrew Press, 1975), p. 213.

Jesus' answer nudges them toward an understanding of His identity—He is letting them know that He is the Messiah, the promised one, in whom they are to place their faith and to whom they are to pledge their allegiance. But the crowd reacts with "prove-it" skepticism.

"What then do You do for a sign, that we may see, and believe You? What work do You perform?" (v. 30)

Recalling the stories they were raised on, this Jewish group digresses from "prove it" to "top this, if you're really who you say you are."

"Our fathers ate the manna in the wilderness; as it is written, 'He gave them bread out of heaven to eat.'" (v. 31)

Jesus makes it clear that Moses wasn't responsible for that wilderness bread, God was. The bread of God was a gift, whether it was shaped into manna or the Messiah (vv. 32–33). Still more attentive to their hunger pangs than to any spiritual pangs of conscience, the crowd would rather have had another loaf of bread than the abundant life within their reach.

They said therefore to Him, "Lord, evermore give us this bread." Jesus said to them, "I am the bread of life; he who comes to Me shall not hunger, and he who believes in Me shall never thirst." (vv. 34–35)

Instead of grasping the gift of salvation offered them, they hold tightly to their skepticism with closed minds and clenched hearts.

"But I said to you, that you have seen Me, and yet do not believe. All that the Father gives Me shall come to Me, and the one who comes to Me I will certainly not cast out. For I have come down from heaven, not to do my own will, but the will of Him who sent Me. And this is the will of Him who sent Me, that of all that He has given Me I lose nothing, but raise it up on the last day. For this is the will of My Father, that everyone who beholds the Son and believes in Him, may have eternal life; and I Myself will raise him up on the last day." (vv. 36–40)

In spite of their rejection, Jesus extends the offer again.

"Truly, truly, I say to you, he who believes has eternal life. I am the bread of life. Your fathers ate the manna in the wilderness, and they died. This is the bread which comes down out of heaven, so that one may eat of it and not die. I am the living bread that came down out of heaven; if anyone eats of this bread, he shall live forever; and the bread also which I shall give for the life of the world is My flesh." (vv. 47–51)

C. Reaction of the multitude. The Jews grumble and argue (vv. 41, 52). No matter how you slice it, it just doesn't set well on their empty stomachs. So they begin to nitpick His sermon.

> The Jews therefore began to argue with one another, saying, "How can this man give us His flesh to eat?" (v. 52)

The mistake is as elemental as one a first-grader might make. Jesus is using a figure of speech, a metaphor. He wasn't literally bread any more than He was literally a lamb or a lion, other symbols used to describe the Messiah. He uses the symbol of bread because the inhabitants of the Ancient Near East saw it as the means for sustaining life (see Deut. 8:3). Patiently, Jesus spells it out for them.

> "Truly, truly, I say to you, unless you eat the flesh of the Son of Man and drink His blood,[2] you have no life in yourselves. He who eats My flesh and drinks My blood has eternal life, and I will raise him up on the last day. For My flesh is true food, and My blood is true drink. He who eats My flesh and drinks My blood abides Me, and I in him. As the living Father sent Me, and ɪ live because of the Father, so he who eats Me, he also shall live because of Me. This is the bread which came down out of heaven; not as the fathers ate, and died, he who eats this bread shall live forever." (vv. 53–58)

III. Personal Impact

At the close of this chapter, we read about three attitudes that parallel responses we see today.

A. Open defection. Many people were attracted to Jesus as a person. They were impressed by His ability to spellbind a crowd with His works and rhetoric. But when the points of His sermon got sharp, these thin-skinned followers recoiled and retreated to the back pews, and some even walked out the doors.

> Many therefore of His disciples, when they heard this said, "This is a difficult statement; who can listen to it?" But Jesus, conscious that His disciples grumbled at this, said to them, "Does this cause you to stumble? What then if you should behold the Son of Man ascending where He was before? It is the Spirit who gives life; the flesh profits nothing; the words that I

---

2. "In Jewish thought *the blood stands for the life.* It is easy to understand why. As the blood flows from a wound, life ebbs away; and to the Jew, *the blood belonged to God. . . .* When Jesus said we must drink his blood he meant that we must take his life into the very core of our hearts." Barclay, *The Gospel of John,* p. 224.

have spoken to you are spirit and are life. But there are some of you who do not believe." For Jesus knew from the beginning who they were who did not believe, and who it was that would betray Him. And He was saying, "For this reason I have said to you, that no one can come to Me, unless it has been granted him from the Father." As a result of this many of His disciples withdrew, and were not walking with Him anymore. (vv. 60–66)

Clearly, the followers described in these verses are unbelievers (vv. 63–64) who found Christ's words difficult to choke down (v. 60).[3]

B. Firm determination. Simon Peter exemplifies the second type of follower.

Jesus said therefore to the twelve, "You do not want to go away also, do you?" Simon Peter answered Him, "Lord, to whom shall we go? You have words of eternal life. And we have believed and have come to know that You are the Holy One of God." (vv. 67–69)

The thinning crowds did nothing to thin the determination of Christ's closest disciples. Rather, their resolve became firmer than ever.

C. Subtle deception. Standing right in the midst of the chosen band of men was one who looked and sounded like the most sincere disciple. His name was Judas, a name which has itself become a metaphor for betrayal.

Jesus answered them, "Did I Myself not choose you, the twelve, and yet one of you is a devil?" Now He meant Judas the son of Simon Iscariot, for he, one of the twelve, was going to betray Him. (vv. 70–71)

Which category do you fall into? Is your life like the grumbling crowd—one of open defection? Or is your life like Judas—one of subtle deception? Or is it like Peter—one of firm determination?

A Concluding Application

As long as Jesus is merely a figure in a book, He remains outside of us. But when we invite Him to enter our hearts, we can feed upon His life and be sustained by the very source of life Himself.

---

3. *Difficult* here means not so much that the saying is vague or hard to understand but that it is hard to accept. The Greek word is *skleros*, meaning "hard to the touch, rough." It is used in James 3:4, speaking of "strong winds," and also in Jude 15, used to describe "harsh things" that were spoken.

William Barclay makes a compelling comparison: Think of it this way. Here in a bookcase is a book which a man has never read. It may be the glory and the wonder of the tragedies of Shakespeare; but so long as it remains unread upon his bookshelves it is external to him. One day he takes it down and reads it. He is thrilled and fascinated and moved. The story sticks to him; the great lines remain in his memory; now when he wants to, he can take that wonder out from inside himself and remember it and think about it and feed his mind and his heart upon it. Once the book was outside him. Now it is inside him and he can feed upon it.[4]

If you've never taken Jesus into your life, assimilated His being into yours, then He is outside of your life. As with a child whose nose is pressed against a bakery store window, it doesn't matter how close you are to the bread or how sweet or fresh you think its smell is. If you don't reach out and take Him as the bread of life, then He's forever encased on the shelf, while you're forever on the street—hungry.

 Living Insights

Study One

The feeding of the five thousand represents the pinnacle of popularity in the earthly ministry of Jesus Christ. Before we move past this important event, let's take some time to analyze it from the perspective of each of the Gospel writers.

- All four gospels give an account of this famous story. Read Matthew 14:13–21, Mark 6:32–44, Luke 9:10–17, and John 6:1–21. Use the space provided to merge the four accounts into one story. Make it as chronologically accurate as possible, and include all the details.

4. Barclay, *The Gospel of John*, p. 224.

The Feeding of the Five Thousand

_____

_____

_____

_____

_____

_____

_____

_____

_____

_____

_____

_____

_____

_____

_____

_____

_____

_____

_____

_____

_____

_____

_____

Continued on next page

📖 Living Insights

The conclusion of this passage shows us the responses of the people to Jesus' message. The three types of responses we read about are still common today.

• Place a check (✔) beside the attitude that best describes your response to Christ.

_____ Open Defection

_____ Firm Determination

_____ Subtle Deception

• Have there been times when you have seen each of the three responses in your life? Describe the ways these attitudes have shown up.

Open Defection _____

_____

_____

_____

_____

Firm Determination _____

_____

_____

_____

_____

Subtle Deception _____

_____

_____

_____

_____

Jesus in the Lions' Den

John 7

As classic as a Shakespearean drama and as edge-of-your-seat exciting as a Spielberg movie, the story of Daniel and the lions' den has captivated both young and old for generations.

Even if you haven't read the story in years, you probably still recall it with technicolor vividness on your mental screen. The protagonist, ninety-year-old Daniel, was framed by a few jealous men in the king's court. Though innocent and faithful, he was thrown into a den of hungry lions. Waiting for the outcome was nerve-shattering: would he be ripped to shreds by the wild lions or would someone, somehow, come to his rescue?

Well, the king, who greatly respected Daniel, couldn't stand the suspense and came to the lions' den early the next morning. To his amazement, Daniel was still alive! God had rescued him, miraculously closing the lions' mouths.

Daniel was not the only one thrown to the lions. Jesus spent the last six months of His life in a lions' den of savages intent on tearing Him to pieces. Eventually these brutal animals cornered Him at the cross (Ps. 23:13). But in our study today, Jesus escapes the enemies' sharp fangs and manages to shut their objecting mouths.

I. Background and Setting

Before we lower ourselves into the lions' den with Jesus and His adversaries, let's get a good look at the scene in its geographic and cultural context.

A. Where? Chapter 7 contains two lions' dens. The first is in Galilee (vv. 1–9), the quiet, safe, familiar home base of Jesus. The other is in Judea (vv. 10–52).

B. Why? With the ill winds of hatred stirring up the inclement weather of opposition against Jesus, talk of assassination eddies about in the air. It's becoming dangerous for Jesus to be seen in Judea (v. 1), and His appearance at the Feast of Tabernacles, or Booths, in Jerusalem must be carefully arranged.

C. When? Bible scholars generally agree that the time setting falls within the last six months of Jesus' life. Verse 2 cues us as to the specific time: "the Feast of Tabernacles was at hand." Israel celebrated three great annual feasts: Passover, Pentecost, and Tabernacles. The latter was held in early October. It was a feast of thanksgiving primarily for the blessings of God in the harvest, but it was also a time of remembering the blessings received during the wilderness wanderings, the time when God manifested Himself in the tabernacle (Lev. 23:33–44). All Jewish males within a twenty-mile radius of Jerusalem were obligated to participate in this festive event, while a multitude of devout Jews from outside the area also attended.

II. People and Reactions

Like Daniel, the Lamb of God finds Himself surrounded by lions—fierce, savage beasts in human form who attack Him intensely and incessantly. This hostile attitude is seen first in His own brothers . . . then in the Jewish people . . . and ultimately in the crowd in general, who, for the most part, reject Him and His message.

A. His brothers. In verses 3–9, the roaring lions are Jesus' own brothers: James, Joseph, Simon, and Judas (compare Matt. 13:55).

> His brothers therefore said to Him, "Depart from here, and go into Judea, that Your disciples also may behold Your works which You are doing. For no one does anything in secret, when he himself seeks to be known publicly. If You do these things, show Yourself to the world." For not even His brothers were believing in Him. (John 7:3–5)[1]

"Hey, bro, if you're such a star, what are you doing here? You should be in Hollywood!" But Jesus responds to their sarcasm with seriousness.

> "My time is not yet at hand, but your time is always opportune. The world cannot hate you; but it hates Me because I testify of it, that its deeds are evil. Go up to the feast yourselves; I do not go up to this feast because My time has not yet fully come." And having said these things to them, He stayed in Galilee. (vv. 6–9)

When Jesus says "My time is not yet at hand," He uses a word that means "season."[2] It is commonly used to refer to the "harvest season" or the "time for figs." The time to reveal Himself is still too green. He must wait till the time is ripe.

B. The Jews. In quiet, unpretentious obscurity, Jesus follows His brothers to the feast (v. 10). But like the most suspenseful of spy novels, the plot thickens as the state officials try to track Jesus down (v. 11). Finally, during the middle of the feast, Jesus makes His identity and whereabouts public—a courageous act in light of the fact that He's a target for assassination.

---

1. The imperfect tense—"were believing"—indicates a continuing attitude.

2. Greek has two words for time: *chronos* and *kairos*. The one used in John 7:6 is *kairos*. Often, it "refers to time not simply in its chronological sequence, but with reference to the events which take place in it. Used in this way, it is time in its qualitative rather than its quantitative aspect. It points to the suitable time, the right time, the favorable opportunity." Leon Morris, *The Gospel According to John* (Grand Rapids, Mich.: William B. Eerdmans Publishing Co., 1971), p. 397.

But when it was now the midst of the feast Jesus went up into the temple, and began to teach. The Jews therefore were marveling, saying, "How has this man become learned, having never been educated?" (vv. 14–15)

The Jewish officials are most concerned about Jesus' credentials. "After all," they must have muttered among themselves, "the guy doesn't even have a seminary degree." They hold an arrogant contempt for this homespun, self-taught storyteller, but His lack of credentials should not be grounds for their dismissal of what He has to say. As commentator William Barclay notes:

> What right had this man to come and lay down the law? Jesus had no cultural background; he had no training in the rabbinic schools and colleges. Surely no intelligent person was going to listen to him? Here was the reaction of academic snobbery.
>
> Many of the greatest poets and writers and evangelists have had no technical qualifications at all. That is not for one moment to say that study and culture and education are to be despised and abandoned; but we must have a care never to wave a man away and consign him to the company who do not matter simply because he lacks the technical equipment of the schools.[3]

C. The crowd. Not only do the skeptical and antagonistic Jewish officials spot Jesus, "the mass viewing audience" also sees Him. And in spite of the overwhelmingly negative reviews of the critics, the multitudes make up their own minds about Him. But this new star, Jesus, doesn't open to rave reviews from them either. Their reaction is mixed (v. 12). Many people are paranoid, as we see in verse 20.

> The multitude answered, "You have a demon! Who seeks to kill You?"

But some have a more courageous attitude (vv. 25–26), and others even believe.

> But many of the multitude believed in Him; and they were saying, "When the Christ shall come, He will not perform more signs than those which this man has, will He?" . . . Others were saying, "This is the Christ." (vv. 31, 41a)

---

3. William Barclay, *The Gospel of John,* vol. 1, rev. ed., The Daily Study Bible Series (Edinburgh, Scotland: Saint Andrew Press, 1975), p. 234.

Because of the diverse opinions about Jesus, tension charges the atmosphere.

So there arose a division in the multitude because of Him. And some of them wanted to seize Him, but no one laid hands on Him. (vv. 43–44)

Although the Jewish officials roar and crouch ready to pounce, they're held at bay—a mute testimony to the fact that there's no lion man can breed that God cannot tame.

III. Jesus and God

Let's focus the spotlight on the lion tamer and how He shuts the mouths of the ravenous beasts that surround Him.

A. The Father. With whip and chair, Jesus stands His ground calmly, with confidence and control—because the ground He stands on is shared with His heavenly Father (vv. 16–18, 33–34).

B. The Spirit. On the last day of the feast, Jesus makes a dramatic statement about Himself (vv. 37–38). But to appreciate the drama of the event, you must understand a little of the ceremonial background to that final day.

Each day of the festival the people came with their palms and their willows to the Temple; with them they formed a kind of screen or roof and marched round the great altar. At the same time a priest took a golden pitcher . . . and went down to the pool of Siloam and filled it with water. It was carried back through the Water Gate while the people recited Isaiah 12:3: "With joy you draw water from the wells of salvation." The water was carried up to the Temple altar and poured out as an offering to God. . . . The whole dramatic ceremony was a vivid thanksgiving for God's good gift of water and an acted prayer for rain, and a memory of the water which sprang from the rock when they travelled through the wilderness.[4]

Against this background, the time is ripe for Jesus to reveal His identity. Dramatically, He stands and shouts:

"If any man is thirsty, let him come to Me and drink. He who believes in Me, as the Scripture said, 'From his innermost being shall flow rivers of living water.' " (vv. 37b–38)

Even knowing that He is opening Himself to attack, Jesus shows His concern for these people's lives. He not only stands up, making Himself an easy target, but He extends His hand to these ruthless lions, offering their lashing tongues the refreshing water of the Holy Spirit.

4. Barclay, *The Gospel of John,* p. 249.

A Lion That Spoke Up

In the peripheral shadows of that lions' den, a voice speaks up in defense of Jesus.

Nicodemus said to them (he who came to Him before, being one of them), "Our Law does not judge a man, unless it first hears from him and knows what he is doing, does it?" (vv. 50–51)

Remember Nicodemus from chapter 3, the Jewish leader who came to Jesus concealed by night? Here we see him take a tentative but definite step out into the open. Finally, by the end of the Gospel, Nicodemus will boldly identify himself with Christ. He, along with Joseph of Arimathea, will take Jesus' ravaged body from the cross and give the Savior a quiet, tender burial (19:38–40).

Little by little, Nicodemus's faith grew, and eventually he came forward ... in an act of love for the Savior, who loved him so patiently and accepted him so readily even though he stood at a distance in the shadows.

Isn't it time you came out of the shadows? Isn't it time you separated from the pack and stepped forward publicly to identify yourself with Jesus? He is calling with outstretched arms: "If any man is thirsty, let him come to Me and drink."

Living Insights

Study One

John 7 is full of rich meat to taste and a wealth of water to drink— more than we could ever touch in a brief lesson. Let's do some further study on our own. This exercise will help us identify the major sections and draw from each some of the themes and truths tucked away in the chapter.

- Who opposed Jesus? Who supported Him? What did He teach? Find your answers in the verses listed.

Verses 1–9

Opposition _____

Support _____

Teachings _____

Continued on next page

_____

_____

Verses 10–13

Opposition _____

Support _____

Teachings _____

_____

_____

Verses 14–24

Opposition _____

Support _____

Teachings _____

_____

_____

Verses 25–31

Opposition _____

Support _____

Teachings _____

_____

_____

Verses 32–36

Opposition _____

Support _____

Teachings _____

_____

_____

Verses 37–39

Opposition _____

Support _____

Teachings _____

_____

_____

Verses 40–44

Opposition _____

Support _____

Teachings _____

_____

_____

Verses 45–53

Opposition _____

Support _____

Teachings _____

_____

_____

📖 *Living Insights*

Study Two ━━

In Study One we began a detailed look at John 7. Let's continue our study on a more personal level.

- Look again at those fifty-three verses, and write down at least one application for each passage.

Verses 1–9

Application _____

_____

Continued on next page

Verses 10–13

Application _____

_____

_____

Verses 14–24

Application _____

_____

_____

Verses 25–31

Application _____

_____

_____

Verses 32–36

Application _____

_____

_____

Verses 37–39

Application _____

_____

_____

Verses 40–44

Application _____

_____

_____

Verses 45–53

Application _____

_____

_____

Letters in the Sand
John 8:1–11

Adultery. According to Old Testament law, it required punishment by death (Lev. 20:10). According to the teachings of Christ in the New Testament, it was legitimate grounds for divorce (Matt. 5:32). Can any sin be as painful, as far-reaching in its consequences, as difficult to forgive?

Of the clandestine thrill of adultery, Solomon poetically writes:

"Stolen water is sweet;
And bread eaten in secret is pleasant." (Prov. 9:17)

But in the very next verse, Solomon focuses on the tragic consequences of entering into such a relationship.

But he does not know that the dead are there,
That her guests are in the depths of Sheol. (v. 18)

Probably no story better illustrates how the sweet, stolen water of adultery turns invariably sour than the story of *Camelot*. In this epic tale, the relationship of King Arthur and Queen Guenevere is trespassed upon when Arthur's most renowned and trusted knight Lancelot gingerly slips his toe across the marital boundary. It started with a look . . . an innocent look, without premeditation or evil intent. But it was a short, slippery step from a look to lust, from infatuation to infidelity. The look eventually led to a touch. The touch sometime later led to a kiss. The kiss, to adultery. And adultery, to tragedy. As George MacDonald writes in his poem "Sweet Peril":

Alas, how easily things go wrong!
A sigh too much, or a kiss too long,
And there follows a mist and a weeping rain,
And life is never the same again.[1]

For the woman in John 8, caught in the very act of adultery, her life, too, would never be the same again. Not because of the stones of judgment ready to be cast at her by the self-righteous crowd of Pharisees, but because of the soft words of forgiveness spoken to her by Jesus.

I. The Setting
The setting is established for us in verses 1–2.

But Jesus went to the Mount of Olives. And early in the morning He came again into the temple, and all the people were coming to Him; and He sat down and began to teach them.

---

1. George MacDonald, "Sweet Peril," as quoted in *The Best Loved Poems of the American People*, selected by Hazel Felleman (Garden City, N.Y.: Garden City Publishing Co., 1936), p. 60.

The morning is like any other Jerusalem morning. It is early; the city is still damp with dew as purple shadows fall among the temple columns. Echoing through the temple are the words of Jesus, who, in rabbinical fashion, sits down to teach the gathered people.

II. The Attack

But suddenly, the serenity of that sacred place is shattered.

A. The interruption.

> And the scribes and the Pharisees brought a woman caught in adultery.... (v. 3)

These scribes and Pharisees are religious leaders bent on destroying Jesus, who poses a threat to their religious oligarchy. Jesus stops teaching; He stares at the men whose voices have been honed on hate. A quick glance at verse 6 reveals that they're acting out a plot that has been rehearsed down to the last detail—a plot so insidious that they are willing to entrap and execute a woman in order to discredit Jesus.

B. The accusation.

With them they drag, like a squirming dog on a leash, a disheveled woman, hastily clothed, barefooted, and humiliated. A woman, they testify, caught in "the very act" of adultery (v. 4). A woman taken abruptly from the bedroom, where she was some man's sexual object, and insensitively dragged to the temple, where she now becomes a political object used to bait the trap set for Jesus.

Dehumanizing People

When we treat people as things, we dehumanize them and destroy something precious inside them. The scribes and Pharisees were not looking at this woman as a person, but as a thing—an instrument whereby they could formulate a charge against Jesus. They were using her as a man might use a worthless pawn in a chess game. To them, she had no name, no personality, no heart, no feelings, no soul. She was simply an expendable pawn in their strategy to corner Jesus into a checkmate.

Whether you use people for your own pleasure or to prove your point, even a religious point, you are treating those people as things to be used instead of human beings to be loved.

C. The question. They set the trap with hair-trigger precision: "Now in the Law Moses commanded us to stone such women; what then do You say?" (v. 5)[2] Judaism's three gravest crimes—idolatry, murder, and adultery— were all punishable by death.

> The *Mishnah*, that is, the Jewish codified law, states that the penalty for adultery is strangulation, and even the method of strangulation is laid down. "The man is to be enclosed in dung up to his knees, and a soft towel set within a rough towel is to be placed around his neck.... Then one man draws in one direction and another in the other direction, until he be dead." The *Mishnah* reiterates that death by stoning is the penalty for a girl who is betrothed and who then commits adultery."[3]

Furthermore, Moses wrote that if the offense took place in a city, both adulterers were to be stoned publicly (Deut. 22:22–24). The appeal in verse 5 is to the Law of Moses, which raises an important question: Where is the guilty man? The accusers testify that the woman was caught "in the very act," so certainly they had equal opportunity to apprehend the man as well. As the pieces of this sordid puzzle begin to fall in place, it is obvious that the scribes and Pharisees did not merely happen by the bedroom window of these clandestine lovers. No, the incident smacks suspiciously of a premeditated trap. Before they could land their trophy fish, they had to first dip their minnow net into the shallows to get their bait. Having caught her, they now hope to hook Christ on the barbs of a dilemma. If He says "Yes, stone her," His compassion for people will be questioned and He will place Himself in jeopardy with the Romans, as only the Roman government can exercise capital punishment. However, if He says "No, release her," He will be accused of not supporting the Law of Moses, thus alienating Himself from the Jews. Essentially, they are staging the same dilemma with the same intent as Mordred, who caught Guenevere and Lancelot in their unfaithfulness. Fighting to get away, Lancelot escaped, but Guenevere was captured and sentenced to death by the court. In the climactic scene where Arthur is called upon to give the signal to commence the execution, Mordred taunts him with wicked joy.

---

2. The Greek text helps capture the emphasis by putting the personal pronoun at the beginning of the sentence. The sense is "*You* now, what's *your* advice?" Clearly, they were trying to place the problem squarely on Jesus.

3. William Barclay, *The Gospel of John,* vol. 2, The Daily Study Bible Series (Edinburgh, Scotland: Saint Andrew Press, 1956), p. 2.

Arthur! What a magnificent dilemma! Let her die, your
life is over; let her live, your life's a fraud. Which will
it be, Arthur? Do you kill the Queen or kill the law?[4]
That's the dilemma. Like Mordred, the Pharisees ask: "What will
it be, Jesus? Do you kill the woman or kill the Law?"

III. The Answer

Between this rock and hard place, Jesus stands firm, refusing to
compromise either His principles or the person for whom those
principles were given.

A. To the men.

And they were saying this, testing Him, in order that
they might have grounds for accusing Him. But Jesus
stooped down, and with His finger wrote on the
ground. But when they persisted in asking Him, He
straightened up, and said to them, "He who is without
sin among you, let him be the first to throw a stone
at her." And again He stooped down, and wrote on
the ground. And when they heard it, they began to
go out one by one, beginning with the older ones,
and He was left alone, and the woman, where she
had been, in the midst. (John 8:6–9)

What Jesus writes in the sand remains a mystery to this day
(v. 6b),[5] but what He says to this self-righteous, self-appointed
judge and jury has echoed throughout the centuries. Deuteronomy
17:7 declared that the witnesses were to be the first to stone the
victim, so Jesus merely forces these legalists to go strictly by
the law. He makes only one qualification: that they take a look
at the log in their own eyes before they try to take the speck
out of somebody else's (Matt. 7:1–5).

B. To the woman.
As if an angel has passed between the helpless
woman and the mob, there is silence; then the vigilantes retreat
home, heads hung in shame—or, at least, in defeat. What a
contrast she and Jesus make: the guilty and the guiltless, adul-
teress and advocate, sinner and Savior.

And straightening up, Jesus said to her, "Woman,
where are they? Did no one condemn you?" And she
said, "No one, Lord." (vv. 10–11a)

---

4. Allen Knee, ed. *Idylls of the King* AND *Camelot* (New York, N.Y.: Dell Publishing Co., 1967),
p. 241.

5. The Greek term used here is not the word normally used for *writing* in the New Testament—
graphō. Rather, it is the word *katagraphō*. Some commentators suggest that Jesus is listing
in the sand the sins of the scribes and Pharisees in order to prick their consciences.

IV. The Counsel

Demonstrating that He is truly "full of grace and truth" (1:14), Jesus forgives the sinner without condoning the sin.

And Jesus said, "Neither do I condemn you; go your way. From now on sin no more." (8:11b)

He cares—"neither do I condemn you"; and He confronts—"sin no more." Undoubtedly, this has been the darkest moment of this woman's life, until the Light of the World bathes her sin in the radiance of His forgiving presence (12:46). The only one supremely qualified to condemn her, doesn't (v. 47).

V. The Principles

From this passage, three truths emerge that we can apply in our relationships today.

A. **The practice of confronting wrong calls for humility, not pride.** Jesus exhorts us in the Sermon on the Mount to look closely at our own lives before we look critically at the lives of others (Matt. 7:5). Paul reiterates this in Galatians 6:1 when he counsels the confronter to be "looking to yourself, lest you too be tempted." The temptation? Pride. If you take the least glimmer of satisfaction in confronting someone else about their sin, that is an indication of pride. Nip it in the bud or you will live to see it grow to overrun your life.

B. **The privilege of condemning wrong is based on righteousness, not knowledge.** Are you "without sin" so that you feel free to cast the first stone (8:7)? Are your eyes without specks so that you can see to take the logs out of the eyes of others (Matt. 7:5)? Are you spiritual enough to restore the one caught in a trespass (Gal. 6:1)? If you're not, then don't (Matt. 7:1–2).

C. **The principle of correcting wrong starts with forgiveness, not rebuke.** Notice the pattern in the way Jesus deals with the guilty woman: "Neither do I condemn you; go your way. From now on sin no more" (John 8:11). Can you imagine a world free from condemnation and judging ... a world marked by forgiveness, not perfection? Just as the journey of a thousand miles begins with the first step, so the task of a world free from judging begins with one person willing to take the first step of compassion and forgiveness. Won't you be that person?

Continued on next page

🐎 Living Insights

The story we've been studying must certainly have been newsworthy that day in Jerusalem. We can well imagine how the story would have read if there had been a *Jerusalem Gazette* at the time.

- Let's pretend there is a *Jerusalem Gazette* and that you are its ace reporter. Reread verses 1–11 and write an article suitable for the front page. Remember the reporter's tools: Who? What? Where? When? Why? and How?

Who? _____

What? _____

Where? _____

When? _____

Why? _____

How? _____

Jerusalem Gazette

Date:	Jerusalem, Judea	Volume:

_____

(Headline)

_____

_____

_____

_____

_____

_____

_____

_____

🦁 *Living Insights*

Study Two

Most of us have spent some time in the sandals of at least one person in this story. Read through the passage again, looking at the people's attitudes and actions concerning *confronting, condemning,* and *correcting.* Then look carefully at your own attitudes and actions.

- What can you learn from the attitudes of the Pharisees and scribes?

- What can you learn from the woman taken in adultery?

- What can you learn from the Lord Jesus?

Reasons for Rejection
John 8:12–59

Dwight L. Moody, by his own admission, made a mistake on the eighth of October 1871—a mistake he determined never to repeat.

He had been preaching in the city of Chicago. That particular night drew his largest audience yet. His message was "What will you do then with Jesus who is called the Christ?"

By the end of the service, he was tired. He concluded his message with a presentation of the gospel and a concluding statement: "Now I give you a week to think that over. And when we come together again, you will have opportunity to respond."

A soloist began to sing. But before the final note, the music was drowned out by clanging bells and wailing sirens screaming through the streets. The great Chicago Fire was blazing. In the ashen aftermath, hundreds were dead and over a hundred thousand were homeless.

Without a doubt, some who heard Moody's message had died in the fire. He reflected remorsefully that he would have given his right arm before he would ever give an audience another week to think over the message of the gospel.

If you were a victim of a fire like that, would you know with certainty whether you would spend eternity with Christ in heaven? Not *hope* or *wish* or *pray* that you would go there—but *know?*

If not, today's study will allow you the opportunity to gain that confidence as we listen in on a debate about the person of Christ and hear His remarkable claims firsthand.

I. The Background and Setting
The background to our passage is the Jewish Feast of Tabernacles (John 7:2), an annual festival of feasting and religious ceremony. The time, apparently, is the day after the final day of the festival. The setting is the temple treasury, where thirteen trumpet-shaped receptacles sat for contributions (8:20). Small at the top and bell-shaped at the bottom, each receptacle required a different offering.

II. Declaration and Response
The verbal sword fight between Jesus and the Pharisees begins in verses 12–13.
A. The radical testimony of Jesus. In verse 12, Jesus begins the fencing match.
> "I am the light of the world; he who follows Me shall not walk in the darkness, but shall have the light of life."

32

The claim is exclusive, one only God could make. Note that Jesus claimed to be *the* light of the world, not *a* light. Although the claim is *ex*clusive, the offer is *in*clusive—an offer any and all could respond to.

B. The rapier thrust of the Pharisees. Responding to the bold claims of Jesus, the Pharisees lash back with a sharp retort. The fencing match is under way.

"You are bearing witness of Yourself; Your witness is not true." (v. 13)

III. Discussion and Debate

Following the initial clash of swords, words fly back and forth in unsheathed passion.

A. General attitudes. The attitude of the Pharisees progressively and heatedly escalates from contradiction (v. 13) to insinuation (v. 19) to denial (v. 33) to insult (v. 48) to sarcasm (v. 53) and, finally and climactically, to violence (v. 59).

B. Specific reasons. Threaded within the fabric of these verses are five specific reasons why the Pharisees rejected the Savior and His words.

1. **Lack of knowledge.** Perhaps the most universal reason for rejecting Jesus is ignorance—an ignorance these Pharisees, along with their ancestors (see Hosea 4:1–3, 6), clearly demonstrate.

   Jesus answered and said to them, "Even if I bear witness of Myself, My witness is true; for I know where I came from, and where I am going; but you do not know where I come from, or where I am going." . . . And so they were saying to Him, "Where is Your Father?" Jesus answered, "You know neither Me, nor My Father; if you knew Me, you would know My Father also." (John 8:14, 19)

2. **Lack of perception.** The Pharisees' lack of perception is brought into focus in verses 15 and 23. Verse 15 highlights their problem, while verse 23 explains why they have it. The problem: "You people judge according to the flesh" (v. 15a). They draw their conclusions from the wrong standard. Looking to externals, they see Jesus only as Joseph's son, the carpenter. They don't have the discernment to see beneath the flesh and blood into the spiritual dimension. The cause: "You are from below . . . you are of this world" (v. 23). Because they have not been born again (3:3), their frame of reference is horizontal rather than vertical (compare Isa. 55:8–9). The inevitable result of such nearsightedness is found in verse 24.

"Unless you believe that I am He, you shall die in your sins."

A Sobering Reality to Face

With a physician's bluntness, Jesus gets right down to the diagnosis: "Terminal cancer. Without radical surgery, you're doomed."

Pretty harsh words. But then again, pretty harsh reality.

If the people who died in the Chicago Fire of 1871 didn't know Christ, they died in their sins and went to an infinitely worse inferno. May I ask you, with a surgeon's frankness: If you died tonight—in a fire, a car wreck, a shooting—would you go to heaven, or would you die in your sins?

---

3. **Lack of appropriation.** Since "faith comes from hearing, and hearing by the word of Christ" (Rom. 10:17), the seed of God's Word plays an essential role in our hearts. There can be no fruit without growth, no growth without life, and no life without a seed. And it is at these Pharisees' fallow hearts that Jesus points His finger.

> "I know that you are Abraham's offspring; yet you seek to kill Me, because My word has no place in you. . . . Why do you not understand what I am saying? It is because you cannot hear My word." (John 8:37, 43)

Remember, now, the Pharisees have majored in religion; they are professionals. Descendants of the great patriarch Abraham, they're also the resident textual and theological experts. But, as John establishes early in his Gospel, we are born into God's family as one of His children, "not of blood, nor of the will of the flesh, nor of the will of man, but of God" (1:13). We become His children by personally receiving Him (v. 12)—not by pedigree, proxy, or pressure.

4. **Lack of desire.** In chapter 8, verses 44 and 45, Jesus lunges His sword into the Pharisees' hearts.

> "You are of your father the devil, and you want to do the desires of your father. He was a murderer from the beginning, and does not stand in the truth, because there is no truth in him. Whenever he speaks a lie, he speaks from his own nature; for he is a liar, and the father of lies. But because I speak the truth, you do not believe Me."

Although the physical lineage of the Pharisees can be traced back to Abraham, their spiritual lineage goes all the way back to the devil himself. In their family tree hid the serpent of old, who had enticed them away from the true God with the seductive apple of religiosity. But under the devil's clerical garb, he is both a murderer and a liar. And, like father, like son, the Pharisees were a mirrored reflection, twisting the truth about Jesus (v. 48) and plotting to kill Him (v. 40).

5. **Lack of humility.** A muscle of pride flexes in verses 52 and 53—the pride of parentage.

> The Jews said to Him, "Now we know that You have a demon. Abraham died, and the prophets also; and You say, 'If anyone keeps My word, he shall never taste of death.' Surely You are not greater than our father Abraham, who died? The prophets died too; whom do You make Yourself out to be?"

This muscle stretches all the way back to the previous discussion. Notice the insinuation in verse 19: "Where is *Your* Father?" (emphasis added). And the innuendo in verse 41: "*We* were not born of fornication" (emphasis added).

IV. Violence and Escape

Appealing to their family tree, Jesus uses the physical parentage of the Pharisees to His advantage.

> "Your father Abraham rejoiced to see My day, and he saw it and was glad." The Jews therefore said to Him, "You are not yet fifty years old, and have You seen Abraham?" Jesus said to them, "Truly, truly, I say to you, before Abraham was born, I am." (vv. 56–58)

Earlier in this Gospel, we saw Jesus claiming "I am the bread of life" (6:48) and "I am the light of the world" (8:12). In 8:58, He says simply, yet dramatically, "I am." In doing so, Jesus claims not only timeless existence but also equality with the God of the Old Testament (compare Exod. 3:14). To the Pharisees, this is blasphemy—a sin that, like adultery, carries the penalty of stoning.

> Therefore they picked up stones to throw at Him; but Jesus hid Himself, and went out of the temple. (John 8:59)

A Final Application

We may either cast stones at Jesus, like the Pharisees, or throw ourselves at His feet, accepting Him as our Lord and Savior.

C. S. Lewis brings the choice into clear focus.

'What are we to make of Christ?'...You must accept or reject the story.

The things He says are very different from what any other teacher has said. Others say, 'This is the truth about the Universe. This is the way you ought to go,' but He says, 'I am the Truth, and the Way, and the Life.' He says, 'No man can reach absolute reality, except through Me.'[1]

Which will it be? Your eternal destiny depends on whether you accept or reject His claims...whether you're clutching stones or clinging to the Savior.

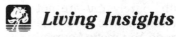 *Living Insights*

Study One

Even a casual reading of John 8 will uncover a progressive attitude of hostility against the Lord Jesus. The anger within the Pharisees eventually erupts at the end of the chapter as they pick up stones to throw at Him.

- Paraphrasing is the art of putting verses of Scripture in your own words. Let's take a closer look at John 8:12–59 by paraphrasing it. Feel free to do a little research and include your findings in your interpretation of the story.

My Paraphrase of John 8:12–59

_____

_____

_____

_____

_____

_____

_____

_____

1. C. S. Lewis, "What Are We to Make of Jesus Christ?" from *God in the Dock: Essays on Theology and Ethics,* ed. Walter Hooper (Grand Rapids, Mich.: William B. Eerdmans Publishing Co., 1970), p. 160.

_____

_____

_____

_____

_____

_____

🐎 *Living Insights*

Study Two ━━━━━━━━━━━━━━━━━━━━━━━━━━━━━━

In this lesson, we saw five reasons why people reject the Lord. Do you know people who refuse Christ because of one of these attitudes? Perhaps you learned something in this lesson that will help you lead these people to Him. Let's prepare the way for Christ to impact their lives by praying for them now.

- Beside each heading below, write down the names of people you know who are using that excuse as a reason for rejection. Conclude this time by praying for each person, asking God to penetrate their lives with the gospel.

Lack of Knowledge _____

_____

Lack of Perception _____

_____

Lack of Appropriation _____

_____

Lack of Desire _____

_____

Lack of Humility _____

_____

Blind Men's Bluff
John 9

Since childhood, Helen Keller grew up blind, deaf, and unable to speak. Yet, through the patient work of one dedicated person, Helen was able to make a meaningful contribution to the world through her writing, teaching, and inspirational example. In her autobiography, Keller records endless days of anticipation and despair, waiting for someone to draw her out. Then she describes the day she first met the person who would do just that—lifelong friend and teacher, Anne Sullivan.

> Have you ever been at sea in a dense fog, when it seemed as if a tangible white darkness shut you in, and the great ship, tense and anxious, groped her way toward the shore with plummet and sounding-line, and you waited with beating heart for something to happen? I was like that ship before my education began, only I was without compass or sounding-line, and had no way of knowing how near the harbour was. "Light! give me light!" was the wordless cry of my soul, and the light of love shone on me in that very hour.

> I felt approaching footsteps. I stretched out my hand as I supposed to my mother. Some one took it, and I was caught up and held close in the arms of her who had come to reveal all things to me, and, more than all things else, to love me.[1]

This tender meeting between teacher and pupil on March 3, 1887, was the turning point of six-year-old Helen's life.

The blind man in John 9 had a similar encounter. For years he sat in the streets, a castaway from society, his soul aching for the touch of light and love. And then one day he heard the approaching footsteps of Jesus, who, with a touch of compassion, gave him new eyes.

I. Case and Cure
Few afflictions are more difficult to bear than blindness. A person without sight is often sentenced to a life of misery and forgotten dreams. Such is the man Jesus sees in the passage we're considering today. Our Lord graciously gives him sight, but because the act is performed on the Jewish Sabbath, the Pharisees are critical. This leads to yet another public conflict between organized, legalistic religion and a vibrant, life-giving relationship with the person of Christ. Toward the end of the chapter it becomes clear that the real blind men are the Pharisees, whose spiritual darkness substitutes the pride of religion for the humility of faith.

1. Helen Keller, *The Story of My Life* (Garden City, N.Y.: Doubleday and Co., 1905), p. 35.

A. The man. The focal point of chapter 9 rests on a beggar with congenital blindness (v. 1)...a man who has never seen the cresting sapphire waves of the Mediterranean surf; never seen the lithely waving arms of blossomed trees in spring; never seen brilliant sunsets shunting their rays of burnished bronze across the Palestinian plain; never seen the awe-inspiring architecture of the temple.

B. The issue. The theological issue is articulated this time not by the scribes and Pharisees but by Jesus' own disciples.

> And His disciples asked Him, saying, "Rabbi, who sinned, this man or his parents, that he should be born blind?" (v. 2)

Their question was logical. In those days, it was commonly taught that a fetus could commit sin while in the mother's womb and that its kicking indicated its sinful state. The Torah, the book of traditional Jewish laws, claimed that it was also possible for God to impose judgment of the parents' iniquity upon their children or grandchildren. We see this happen today when venereal diseases and alcoholism pass on birth defects to the next generation. Like medieval theologians who argued over how many angels could fit on the head of a pin, these fledgling seminarians were moved to theological controversy rather than tenderhearted compassion. But instead of scolding His students, Jesus gives them a short lecture on Christology.

> "It was neither that this man sinned, nor his parents; but it was in order that the works of God might be displayed in him. We must work the works of Him who sent Me, as long as it is day; night is coming, when no man can work. While I am in the world, I am the light of the world." (vv. 3–5)

C. The miracle. The Bible records three times that Jesus used saliva to effect a miracle: in Mark 7:33 and 8:23, and here in verses 6–7 of John 9.

> When He had said this, He spat on the ground, and made clay of the spittle, and applied the clay to his eyes, and said to him, "Go, wash in the pool of Siloam" (which is translated, Sent). And so he went away and washed, and came back seeing.

Questions shoot up their hands and wave for an answer—Why clay? Why spittle? Why the pool of Siloam? But they are drowned out by the jubilation of the beggar returning from the pool, seeing for the first time in his life.

Helen Keller tells of the dramatic moment when Annie Sullivan first broke through her dark, silent world with the illumination of language.

> We walked down the path to the well-house, attracted by the fragrance of the honeysuckle with which it was covered. Some one was drawing water and my teacher placed my hand under the spout. As the cool stream gushed over one hand she spelled into the other the word *water,* first slowly, then rapidly. I stood still, my whole attention fixed upon the motions of her fingers. Suddenly I felt a misty consciousness as of something forgotten—a thrill of returning thought; and somehow the mystery of language was revealed to me. I knew then that "w-a-t-e-r" meant the wonderful cool something that was flowing over my hand. That living word awakened my soul, gave it light, hope, joy, set it free! There were barriers still, it is true, but barriers that could in time be swept away.[2]

Certainly, this was how the blind man must have felt when he saw water for the first time as he washed his eyes in the pool of Siloam.

Just as the Light of the world gave sight to the blind beggar, and just as that "living word" awakened the soul of Helen Keller, so Jesus can awaken your life with the tender touch of His hand. He can give you light, hope, joy, and freedom like you've never known before. Surely there will still be barriers in your life—but barriers that can be swept away in time.

II. Questions and Answers

What happens when the Light of the world meets a dimly burning wick of humanity (Isa. 42:3)? Does He rebuke it for its faint flicker? Does He snuff it out? No. Jesus tenderly takes the charred wick in His hand and kindles its flame. But the physical light Jesus brings to this man is only a glimmer of the spiritual light that will soon follow.

A. **Between neighbors and beggar.** Like reporters at a presidential press conference, the neighbors ply the beggar with questions (John 9:8–11). His answer is unadorned and unembellished, dressed only in the truth.

2. Keller, *The Story of My Life,* p. 36.

40

And they said to him, "Where is He?" He said, "I do not know." (v. 12)

B. Between Pharisees and beggar. The following passage perfectly illustrates how "the light shines in the darkness; and the darkness did not comprehend it" (1:5).

They brought to the Pharisees him who was formerly blind. Now it was a Sabbath on the day when Jesus made the clay, and opened his eyes. Again, therefore, the Pharisees also were asking him how he received his sight. And he said to them, "He applied clay to my eyes, and I washed, and I see." Therefore some of the Pharisees were saying, "This man is not from God, because He does not keep the Sabbath." (vv. 13–16a)

Juxtaposed to the newfound physical sight of the beggar is the utter spiritual blindness of the religious aristocracy. Instead of sharing the joy of a person made whole, the Pharisees grind their teeth because the miracle took place on the Sabbath.[3] But the debate soon shifts the focus from the issue of the Sabbath to the identity of this enigmatic miracle worker.

But others were saying, "How can a man who is a sinner perform such signs?" And there was a division among them. They said therefore to the blind man again, "What do you say about Him, since He opened your eyes?" And he said, "He is a prophet." (vv. 16b–17)

But the Jews, blind to the miracle (v. 18), interrogate the beggar's parents (vv. 19–21). Intimidated by this cross-examination and afraid of being excommunicated, the parents plead ignorance (vv. 21–23). So the Pharisees return the beggar to the witness stand.

So a second time they called the man who had been blind, and said to him, "Give glory to God; we know that this man is a sinner." He therefore answered, "Whether He is a sinner, I do not know; one thing I do know, that, whereas I was blind, now I see." (vv. 24–25)

---

3. By this time, years of legalistic accretion had encrusted the original Sabbath laws like barnacles. If a lamp ran out of oil, for example, you couldn't fill it on the Sabbath. If sandals were shod with nails, you couldn't walk in them. You couldn't trim your moustache or hair or even a fingernail. And benevolent acts like setting a broken bone had to be postponed till after the Sabbath. It is obvious that by the time of Christ something had gone awry with Sabbath observance. Jesus Himself indicated that the intent of the Sabbath regulations had been turned around 180 degrees when He declared that "the Sabbath was made for man, and not man for the Sabbath" (Mark 2:27). For other verbal altercations Jesus had with the Pharisees over this issue, see Matthew 12:1–8 and Luke 13:10–17, 14:1–6.

The Mute Eloquence of a Changed Life

No testimony is quite as compelling as that of a changed life. People can argue theology and dispute interpretations of the Bible, but they are rendered speechless when confronted with the reality of a changed life. It is the unarguable apologetic. Cardinal Suhard gives us a convicting definition of such a life:

> To be a witness does not consist in engaging in propaganda, nor even in stirring people up, but in being a living mystery. It means to live in such a way that one's life would not make sense if God did not exist.[4]

Certainly this could be said of the blind man's life after he met Jesus . . . and of so many people whom Jesus touched. Can it be said of you? Is your life a cold monument to religious duty—or is it "a living mystery"?

The Pharisees continue their attack not only by denigrating Jesus (v. 24) but also by sarcastically discrediting the man Jesus has healed: "You were born entirely in sins, and are you teaching us?" (v. 34). This severe rebuke is prompted by the man's insightful comments in verses 30–33.

> The man answered and said to them, "Well, here is an amazing thing, that you do not know where He is from, and yet He opened my eyes. We know that God does not hear sinners; but if anyone is God-fearing, and does His will, He hears him. Since the beginning of time it has never been heard that anyone opened the eyes of a person born blind. If this man were not from God, He could do nothing."

III. Belief and Unbelief

Although the Pharisees cast the man out of the temple, the Lord of the temple seeks him out, and for the first time the man born blind beholds the Light of the world face-to-face.

> Jesus heard that they had put him out; and finding him, He said, "Do you believe in the Son of Man?" He answered and said, "And who is He, Lord, that I may believe in Him?" Jesus said to him, "You have both seen Him, and He is the one who is talking with you." And he said, "Lord, I believe." And he worshiped Him. And Jesus said, "For judgment I came into this world, that those who do not

---

4. As quoted by Madeleine L'Engle, *Walking on Water: Reflections on Faith and Art* (Wheaton, Ill.: Harold Shaw Publishers, 1980), p. 31.

see may see; and that those who see may become blind."
Those of the Pharisees who were with Him heard these
things, and said to Him, "We are not blind too, are we?"
Jesus said to them, "If you were blind, you would have
no sin; but since you say, 'We see,' your sin remains."
(vv. 35–41)
"John evidently wants us to see that the activity of Jesus as the Light
of the world inevitably results in judgment for those whose natural
habitat is darkness."[5] The other side to that coin is the restoration
of sight to those who admit to their darkened condition and come
out, as the blind man did, to embrace the light.

┌─ *A Concluding Application* ─────────────────────────
│   Helen Keller nostalgically recalls her feelings about that
│ life-changing day when she first met Annie Sullivan.
│   I learned a great many new words that day. I do
│   not remember what they all were; but I do know that
│   *mother, father, sister, teacher* were among them—
│   words that were to make the world blossom for me,
│   "like Aaron's rod, with flowers." It would have been
│   difficult to find a happier child than I was as I lay
│   in my crib at the close of that eventful day and lived
│   over the joys it had brought me, and for the first
│   time longed for a new day to come.[6]
│ Jesus can do that for your life. He'll make it blossom. Give
│ you joy. Give you a reason to live—a longing for a new day to
│ come. The Word that became flesh can incarnate Himself in
│ your life and fill every dark corner with light.
└──

Living Insights

Study One ▬▬▬▬▬▬▬▬▬▬▬▬▬▬▬▬▬▬▬▬▬▬▬▬▬▬▬▬
    The man born blind gave Christ an excellent opportunity to heal
and to teach the truth about spiritual sight and spiritual blindness.
Let's use the text's many questions and answers to gain greater insight
into the teaching.

Continued on next page

---

5. Leon Morris, *The Gospel According to John* (Grand Rapids, Mich.: William B. Eerdmans
Publishing Co., 1971), p. 483.
6. Keller, *The Story of My Life*, p. 37.

- At least a dozen questions are asked in this ninth chapter of John. As you reread these verses, record the questions and answers in the space provided.

John 9

Verse _____

Question _____

_____

Answer _____

_____

Verse _____

Question _____

_____

Answer _____

_____

Verse _____

Question _____

_____

Answer _____

_____

Verse _____

Question _____

_____

Answer _____

_____

Verse _____

Question _____

_____

Answer _____

_____

Verse _____

Question _____

_____

Answer _____

_____

Verse _____

Question _____

_____

Answer _____

_____

Verse _____

Question _____

_____

Answer _____

_____

Verse _____

Question _____

_____

Answer _____

_____

Verse _____

Question _____

_____

Answer _____

_____

Verse _____

Question _____

Continued on next page

Answer _____

_____

Verse _____

Question _____

_____

Answer _____

_____

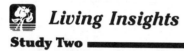 *Living Insights*

Study Two ▬▬▬▬▬▬▬▬▬▬▬▬▬▬▬▬▬▬▬▬▬▬▬▬▬▬▬

   Have you ever thought about what it really means to have Christ as your Light? The entire concept of light is rich in spiritual symbolism. It is worth a few minutes of our time to consider how the Light impacts us in a personal way.

● What evidence do you see of the Light in your life? What difference does He make in the way you live? Jot down your thoughts on this issue.

Evidence of the Light in My Life

_____

_____

_____

_____

_____

_____

_____

The Living Door
John 10

The Old Testament often depicts God as the shepherd of His people. The New Testament uses the same image for Jesus.[1]

There is no better loved picture of Jesus than the picture of Him as the Good Shepherd. The picture of the shepherd is deeply woven into the language and the imagery of the Bible. It could not be otherwise. The main part of Judaea is a central plateau. It stretches from Bethel to Hebron for a distance of about 35 miles. It varies from 14 to 17 miles across. The ground, for the most part, is rough and stony. Judaea was, therefore, naturally much more a pastoral than an agricultural country. It was, therefore, inevitable that the most familiar figure of the Judaean uplands was the shepherd. The life of the Palestinian shepherd was very hard. In Palestine no flock ever grazes without a shepherd, and the shepherd is never off duty. There is little grass, and the sheep are bound to wander far afield. There are no protecting walls, and the sheep have ever to be watched. On either side of the narrow plateau the ground dips sharply down to the craggy deserts and the sheep are always liable to wander away and to get lost. The shepherd's task was constant and dangerous, for, in addition, he had to guard the flock against wild animals, especially against wolves, and there were ever thieves and robbers ready to steal the sheep.[2]

In John 10, we'll see how this backdrop helps bring the words of Jesus into sharp relief.

I. The Teaching of Jesus
In Palestine sheep were kept primarily for their wool rather than for food. Thus sheep were usually with a shepherd for years and were often known by descriptive names like "Brown-leg" or "Black-ear." The sheep were suspicious of strangers, but each sheep knew and understood its shepherd's voice and followed whenever that shepherd called. In the villages, communal sheepfolds sheltered the flocks when they returned home at night. These folds were protected by a strong door to which only the guardian of the door held the key.

A. The instruction. With this understanding, the words of Jesus in John 10:1–5 take on greater clarity and color.

---

1. Old Testament examples would be Psalms 23, 77:20, 79:13 and Isaiah 40:11. In the New Testament, Matthew 9:36, 18:12, 26:31 and 1 Peter 2:25 are places where this image can be found.

2. William Barclay, *The Gospel of John,* vol. 2, The Daily Study Bible Series (Edinburgh, Scotland: Saint Andrew Press, 1956), p. 61.

"Truly, truly, I say to you, he who does not enter by the door into the fold of the sheep, but climbs up some other way, he is a thief and a robber. But he who enters by the door is a shepherd of the sheep. To him the doorkeeper opens, and the sheep hear his voice, and he calls his own sheep by name, and leads them out. When he puts forth all his own, he goes before them, and the sheep follow him because they know his voice. And a stranger they simply will not follow, but will flee from him, because they do not know the voice of strangers."

B. The interpretation. The disciples are confused by the parable (v. 6), so Jesus patiently offers them a simple explanation.

"Truly, truly, I say to you, I am the door of the sheep. All who came before Me are thieves and robbers, but the sheep did not hear them. I am the door; if anyone enters through Me, he shall be saved, and shall go in and out, and find pasture. The thief comes only to steal, and kill, and destroy; I came that they might have life, and might have it abundantly. I am the good shepherd; the good shepherd lays down His life for the sheep. He who is a hireling, and not a shepherd, who is not the owner of the sheep, beholds the wolf coming, and leaves the sheep, and flees, and the wolf snatches them, and scatters them. He flees because he is a hireling, and is not concerned about the sheep. I am the good shepherd; and I know My own, and My own know Me, even as the Father knows Me and I know the Father; and I lay down My life for the sheep." (vv. 7–15)

During warm weather, the sheep were not driven back to the village but collected for the night into rustic, makeshift sheep-folds on the hillside.

These hillside sheep-folds were just open spaces enclosed by a wall. In them there was an opening by which the sheep came in and went out; but there was no door of any kind. What happened was that at night the shepherd himself lay down across the opening and entrance, and no sheep could get out or in except over his body. In the most literal sense the shepherd was the door; there was no access to the sheep-fold except through him.[3]

3. Barclay, *The Gospel of John,* p. 67.

It is clear from His interpretation that Jesus is the door and that there is no other way into the fold but through Him (v. 9; compare 14:6). No doubt, "doorkeeper" in verse 3 refers to the Holy Spirit. "Thieves and robbers" probably refers to pseudo-messiahs (vv. 1, 8, 10). And the "hireling" of verses 12 and 13 obviously stands for the Pharisees and scribes.

C. **The revelation.** The sheep mentioned throughout chapter 10 are divided into two groups, "the fold of the sheep" (v. 1) and "other sheep, which are not of this fold" (v. 16).

> "And I have other sheep, which are not of this fold; I must bring them also, and they shall hear My voice; and they shall become one flock with one shepherd. For this reason the Father loves Me, because I lay down My life that I may take it again. No one has taken it away from Me, but I lay it down on My own initiative. I have authority to lay it down, and I have authority to take it up again. This commandment I received from My Father." (vv. 16–18)

These two distinct groups of sheep symbolize two separate bodies of believers. The "fold" is clearly a reference to those of Jewish ancestry who had accepted Jesus as their Messiah. The "other sheep," then, would be the Gentile believers. The two groups would become one fold, but only through the sacrificial death of the shepherd (compare Gal. 3:28).

─ *The Story of the Good Shepherd* ─────

The story of the Good Shepherd is not the tragic story of a victim but the tremendous story of a victor—one who secured His victory by voluntarily laying His life down on our behalf.

Pilate tried to intimidate Jesus with the authority to release Him or crucify Him (John 19:10). Peter tried to protect Him with his sword at Gethsemane (Matt. 26:51; compare John 18:10). But Jesus' death was voluntary. He told Peter, "Put your sword back into its place. . . . Or do you think that I cannot appeal to My Father, and He will at once put at My disposal more than twelve legions of angels?" (Matt. 26:52–53). And to Pilate, Jesus replied, "You would have no authority over Me, unless it had been given you from above" (John 19:11).

No, Jesus did not become entrapped in some sticky political web from which He could not extricate Himself. Rather, He spun a story of selfless sacrifice so enticing, so enchanting that it would attract people to Him for millennia to come.

And we, those "other sheep," have come into the fold because that two-thousand-year-old story stirred us like nothing else—that story of a shepherd so supremely good that nothing stood in the way of His love for His sheep.

Not even His own life.

II. The Reaction of the Jews

The Jews' reactions are mixed (v. 19): some hate Jesus, castigating Him as satanic or psychotic (v. 20); others, though as yet uncommitted, are convinced His words and deeds could not be attributed to demonic power (v. 21). The dissension remains unresolved as the curtain abruptly falls on this scene.

III. The Hostile Discussion

The curtain reopens to a winter set during the Feast of the Dedication in Jerusalem.

A. The setting. The scene is Solomon's porch (vv. 22–23), elegantly roofed and colonnaded with magnificent forty-foot stone pillars. Here rabbis walk with their students, discussing and debating the hot theological issues of the day.

B. The dialogue. Jesus picks up where He left off—in a discussion revolving around the question of His identity. Jesus appeals to His works and His words, claiming that only the Messiah could perform the deeds He has done.

> The Jews therefore gathered around Him, and were saying to Him, "How long will You keep us in suspense? If You are the Christ, tell us plainly." Jesus answered them, "I told you, and you do not believe; the works that I do in My Father's name, these bear witness of Me. But you do not believe, because you are not of My sheep. My sheep hear My voice, and I know them, and they follow Me; and I give eternal life to them, and they shall never perish; and no one shall snatch them out of My hand. My Father, who has given them to Me, is greater than all; and no one is able to snatch them out of the Father's hand. I and the Father are one." (vv. 24–30)

Jesus' use of sheep imagery in verses 26–29 provides us with four qualities of genuine believers: they are sensitive to His voice, obedient to His leadership, confident of their destiny, and secure in the shepherd's strong and loving arms.

C. The rejection. But the response of these Jews indicates that they are recalcitrant goats rather than compliant sheep. For instead of running to the shepherd like lost sheep, they prefer to butt heads with Him like stubborn nanny goats (vv. 31–39). The question of Jesus' identity is unambiguously settled, but they will not accept it. With stones in hand, this Jewish jury declares His sentence: "For a good work we do not stone You, but for blasphemy; and because You, being a man, make Yourself out to be God" (v. 33).

Genuine Reception

John tells us earlier in his Gospel that Jesus "came to His own, and those who were His own did not receive Him" (1:11). He came to shepherd a wayward bunch of rebel goats, but they lowered their stubborn heads and pawed the ground in opposition to Him.

Now, most probably, you are not a goat but a sheep. But what kind of sheep are you?

Are you sensitive to His voice when He speaks to you in His Word? How about when He speaks to you through your conscience? Or through other people? God spoke to Balaam through a donkey. Certainly, He could speak to you through an obstinate acquaintance . . . or through a strong-willed child . . . or through some circumstance that has plopped itself smack-dab in front of you, staring you stubbornly in the face.

Are you obedient to His voice? It's one thing to hear; it's quite another thing to act on what you've heard. His sheep are to be not only hearers but doers of His word as well (James 1:22–25).

Are you confident in your destiny? Are you secure in your relationship with Christ? Remember, you're in the Good Shepherd's invincible hands—hands that even Satan himself cannot pry open!

Living Insights

Study One

In today's high-tech society, it would be out of the ordinary for a child to say, "When I grow up, I wanna be a shepherd!" Yet the keeping of sheep was a very common occupation in New Testament Judea. And there's no better description than in John 10.

Continued on next page

- Because John 10 is quite familiar to many of us, perhaps a fresh look at this chapter is in order. Find a different version of the Scriptures and reread the chapter. Maybe a paraphrase like the Living Bible or The New Testament in Modern English, by J. B. Phillips, would be helpful. Record your discoveries in the following space.

A New Look at John 10

_____

_____

_____

_____

_____

_____

Living Insights

Study Two ▬▬▬▬▬▬▬▬▬▬▬▬▬▬▬▬▬▬▬▬▬▬▬

When discussing the relationship between the shepherd and the sheep, we usually give most of our attention to the shepherd. However, our study included four characteristics of sheep. How well do you measure up, fellow sheep? Use the questions below to rate yourself, 5 being the highest rating. Then, in the space that follows, create a strategy for improvement in your areas of greatest need.

- How sensitive am I to Christ's voice?   1 2 3 4 5

- How obedient am I to Christ's leadership?   1 2 3 4 5

- How confident am I of my destiny?   1 2 3 4 5

- How secure do I feel in Christ's care?   1 2 3 4 5

How I Can Be a Better Sheep

_____

_____

_____

_____

Back from Beyond
John 11

Death is usually the last thing we want to talk about. It makes us feel uncomfortable, awkward. We recoil when someone brings the subject up, as if a flaming torch were shoved in our face.

One of the reasons we fear death is that, in spite of all our medical achievements, we haven't been able to conquer it.

> The hearse began its grievous journey many thousand years ago, as a litter made of saplings.
>
> Litter, sled, wagon, Cadillac: the conveyance has changed, but the corpse it carries is the same. Birth and death enclose man in a sort of parenthesis of the present. And the brackets at the beginning and end of life are still impenetrable.
>
> This frustrates us, especially in a time of scientific break-through and exploding knowledge, that we should be able to break out of earth's environment and yet be stopped cold by death's unyielding mystery. Electroencephalogram may replace mirror held before the mouth, autopsies may become more so-phisticated, cosmetic embalming may take the place of pennies on the eyelids and canvas shrouds, but death continues to con-front us with its blank wall. Everything changes; death is change-less.
>
> We may postpone it, we may tame its violence, but death is still there waiting for us.
>
> Death always waits. The door of the hearse is never closed.[1]

Today we are going to penetrate, however slightly, that unyielding mys-tery. We're going to examine the account of a man raised from the dead—a man who came back from beyond.

I. The Sickness of Lazarus
About two miles outside of Jerusalem lay the sleepy hamlet of Bethany, a parenthesis of peace where Jesus often found rest and relaxation in the home of Lazarus and his two sisters, Martha and Mary. But all is not peaceful this particular day—Lazarus is deathly ill (John 11:1–2). In desperation, the sisters send for Jesus.

"Lord, behold, he whom You love is sick." (v. 3)

II. The Response of Jesus
Verse 5 reveals that "Jesus loved Martha, and her sister, and Lazarus." In light of that, you would expect Jesus to drop everything and come

---

1. Joseph Bayly, *The Last Thing We Talk About,* rev. ed. (Elgin, Ill.: David C. Cook Publishing Co., 1973), p. 11.

running to Lazarus's bedside. But curiously, Jesus delays for two days (v. 6). Was He too busy? Was He attending to other matters of greater importance? No. The purpose for the delay was twofold: one, "for the glory of God, that the Son of God may be glorified by it" (v. 4); and two, "so that you may believe" (v. 15).

Coping with Crisis

In times of crisis, it is essential that we understand some important facts about *time* and *perspective*.

Regarding time, our Lord is never late. He often delays His response, but He is never late. His watch is merely set to a different timetable, calibrated to matters of eternal consequence rather than temporal.

Regarding perspective, we can adopt either a human or a divine outlook. The human perspective focuses on the urgent and blurs the important. It concentrates on our immediate welfare rather than our ultimate welfare, on our temporary good instead of God's eternal glory. The divine perspective, however, factors eternity into the enigmatic equations of life. While the human perspective pleads, *"My will be done, now,"* the divine perspective makes its request, yet patiently adds "Nevertheless, not my will be done, but Thine."

How is your vision and sense of divine timing during trials? Do you see only the crisis—or do you see Christ's hand behind, before, below, above, and within that crisis? And have you checked your spiritual watch lately? Is it synchronized with eternity? Is it keeping His time—or your own?

III. The Reactions of Mary and Martha

By the time Jesus finally comes to Bethany, Lazarus has died and has been in the tomb for four days (v. 17). Christ's arrival sparks reactions in Mary and Martha—reactions that are both similar and dissimilar. Note the contrast in verse 20:

Martha therefore, when she heard that Jesus was coming, went to meet Him; but Mary still sat in the house.

But notice the similarity of their initial greetings. First Martha's:

"Lord, if You had been here, my brother would not have died." (v. 21)

Then Mary's:

Therefore, when Mary came where Jesus was, she saw Him, and fell at His feet, saying to Him, "Lord, if You had been here, my brother would not have died." (v. 32)

Although their words are the same, their posture is not. Martha runs to Him, erect; Mary falls at His feet, prostrate. Angry, hurt, confused, and crushed, Martha engages Jesus in a theological debate.

"Even now I know that whatever You ask of God, God will give You." Jesus said to her, "Your brother shall rise again." Martha said to Him, "I know that he will rise again in the resurrection on the last day." Jesus said to her, "I am the resurrection and the life; he who believes in Me shall live even if he dies, and everyone who lives and believes in Me shall never die. Do you believe this?" (vv. 22–26)

With this question reaching out to her, Martha softens, grasping the truth with open arms.

She said to Him, "Yes, Lord; I have believed that You are the Christ, the Son of God, even He who comes into the world." (v. 27)

Martha needed intellectual buttressing, but Mary needs emotional support.

When Jesus therefore saw her weeping, and the Jews who came with her, also weeping, He was deeply moved in spirit, and was troubled, and said, "Where have you laid him?" They said to Him, "Lord, come and see." Jesus wept. And so the Jews were saying, "Behold how He loved him!" (vv. 33–36)

Martha needed to know that Jesus was in control. Mary needed to know that Jesus cared. And without rebukes or reservations, He met each sister where she was, whether standing or prostrate and whether needing intellectual support or emotional.

If Only

Those two regretful words. How broad the blame that's placed on their narrow shoulders!

"If only we hadn't moved here ..."

"If only I hadn't married him ..."

"If only I hadn't listened to her ..."

"If only we had more money ..."

What are your "if onlys"? Won't you take them to Jesus, like Mary and Martha did? Let Him assure you, as He did those forlorn sisters, that He is in control—and that He cares.

IV. The Raising of Lazarus

Jesus then comes to the tomb, that stone testimony of a creation gone tragically awry. And again He grieves (v. 38). Tersely, with restrained anger at the briared wilderness Satan has made of His edenic creation, Jesus instructs the onlookers: "Remove the stone" (v. 39a). Once the stone is removed, Jesus prays (vv. 41–42), then shouts: "Lazarus, come forth" (v. 43). And, like an eerie scene from *The Mummy's Tomb,* Lazarus comes forth—back from beyond (v. 44). The surrounding crowd has just witnessed a dead man called to life. But their response to this miracle is mixed. There is belief (v. 45), as the Lord had prayed (v. 42), and there is disbelief and deceit (vv. 46–57).

V. Two Truths for Today

After that, Lazarus must have been the talk of the town—front page news in the *Bethany Times.* He became known, for sure, as the one who came back from beyond. What stories he could have told! From this dramatic event that quaked the Judean countryside, two tremors of truth ripple through the centuries to touch our lives today.

   A. **When delay occurs, God has a better time and a better way.**

   B. **When death occurs, God has a better plan and a better purpose.**

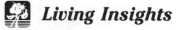 *Living Insights*

Study One ▬▬▬▬▬▬▬▬▬▬▬▬▬▬▬▬▬▬▬▬▬▬

The raising of Lazarus from the dead is one of Christ's most captivating miracles, perhaps because of the stunning contrast of life reigning victorious over death. Dealing with death is never easy, yet we must be prepared for it.

• First Corinthians 15 is essential reading for anyone dealing with death. Turn your attention to this great text by carefully reading the entire chapter. As thoughts come to mind on death, jot them down in the space below.

Dealing with Death—1 Corinthians 15

Verse: _____   Comment: _____

_____

Verse: _____   Comment: _____

_____

Verse: _____   Comment: _____

_____

Verse: _____ Comment: _____

_____

Verse: _____ Comment: _____

_____

Verse: _____ Comment: _____

_____

Verse: _____ Comment: _____

_____

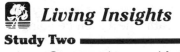 *Living Insights*

Study Two ▬▬▬▬▬▬▬▬▬▬▬▬▬▬▬▬▬▬▬▬▬▬▬

Our experiences with tragedy and death may not seem as exciting as the ones in the lesson, but they are no less significant. Using our lesson's two concluding principles, reflect on your own circumstances. In the space provided, express how you have experienced these two truths.

• When delay occurs, God has a better time and a better way.

_____

_____

_____

_____

_____

• When death occurs, God has a better plan and a better purpose.

_____

_____

_____

_____

_____

Seeking before Hiding
John 12

From his days on the pediatric staff of USC Medical Center in Los Angeles, Dr. James Dobson tells the story of a five-year-old boy dying of lung cancer. Many parents of terminally ill children can't handle the pressure and grief and, consequently, let them die alone. But this little boy's mother came to his hospital room every day, holding him, rocking him, loving him.

One night, after the mother had gone home, the nurses heard the child talking in his room, saying over and over, "I hear the bells! I hear the bells! They're ringing!" They assumed he was hallucinating and told his mother so the next morning.

"He was not hallucinating," she replied. "Weeks ago, I told my boy that when the pain got so bad that he couldn't breathe, he'd soon be going to heaven to be with Jesus. And when that pain got too bad, he was to look up toward heaven and listen for the bells. They'd be ringing. They'd be ringing for him."

With that, she turned into his room, gathered her son in her arms, and rocked him into the waiting arms of God.

What a picture of peace. That mother and son could face death because they had security in Jesus Christ. They had accepted His plan.

In John 12, Jesus begins his last week on earth. Pain, rejection, and death await Him, yet He can face it all because He has accepted God's plan, "entrusting Himself to Him who judges righteously" (1 Pet. 2:23).

I. A Survey of the Final Week

After Jesus brought Lazarus back to life, the infuriated Pharisees made serious plans to kill Him. To escape their wrath, He fled with His disciples to Ephraim, a remote city north of Jerusalem, on the edge of the Judean desert (John 11:53–54). At this juncture, Jesus begins to alter His ministry. First, He changes His public outreach to a private one—He moves from seeking the multitudes to sequestering Himself with the disciples (see 12:36b). Second, He shifts His emphasis away from miracles and concentrates on quiet, intimate conversation with His twelve men (chaps. 13–17). In fact, the raising of Lazarus is the last miracle until His own Resurrection. And third, He reduces His travels, returning to Jerusalem and staying there (12:12). He's not out evangelizing; He's preparing to leave and preparing the disciples for His departure.

> **What about Your Last Week?**
> If you knew you had only one more week to live, how would
> you spend your time? What's really important to you? Look
> closely at Christ's last days before the cross. He chose to spend
> His final moments with those most dear, with His closest friends.
> This week, this day, could be your last. How are you investing
> your time?

II. A Study of the First Part of the Week

As this last week unfolds, the things Jesus does and says are of top
priority. He's still in the public eye at the beginning of the week, and
John captures three events in his twelfth chapter.

A. Six days before (vv. 1–11). After His sojourn in Ephraim, Jesus
is back in Bethany as the guest of honor at a dinner party. Re-
laxing around the table with Him are the disciples and Lazarus.
While Martha serves them, Mary enters the room with a dramatic gesture.

> Mary therefore took a pound of very costly perfume
> of pure nard, and anointed the feet of Jesus, and
> wiped His feet with her hair; and the house was filled
> with the fragrance of the perfume.[1] (v. 3)

Mary performs this worshipful act of love with no regard for
appearance. Respectable Jewish women never let their hair
down in public, nor did they sit around the dinner table with
Jewish men. But Judas, in faulting her behavior, doesn't condemn her for those things; he condemns her extravagance.

> "Why was this perfume not sold for three hundred
> denarii, and given to poor people?" (v. 5)

That sounds noble, doesn't it? But in the sixty years between
Judas's act and the time this book was written, John has learned
that Judas's response was not so pure.

> Now he said this, not because he was concerned
> about the poor, but because he was a thief, and as
> he had the money box, he used to pilfer what was
> put into it. (v. 6)

Judas is the treasurer for the disciples, the most trusted man in
the group. But Jesus, who sees fully the betrayal in Judas's heart
(see v. 4), defends Mary's selfless devotion.

1. "Many scholars have seen a double meaning here. They have taken this sentence to mean
that the whole Church was filled with the sweet memory of Mary's lovely deed. A lovely deed
becomes the possession of the whole world. It adds something to the beauty of life in general.
A lovely deed brings into the world something permanently precious, something which time
cannot ever take away." William Barclay, *The Gospel of John*, vol. 2, The Daily Study Bible
Series (Edinburgh, Scotland: Saint Andrew Press, 1956), p. 129.

"Let her alone, in order that she may keep it for the day of My burial. For the poor you always have with you, but you do not always have Me." (vv. 7–8)

Mary is preparing Jesus' body for burial, while Judas prepares His death.

The Other Guest

John says that this dinner party is for Jesus (v. 2), but another guest draws quite a bit of attention. In verse 9, we see that a great multitude has gathered outside the house, not just to see Jesus, "but that they might also see Lazarus, whom He raised from the dead."

Lazarus is a living miracle, and, by merely living, he's spreading the gospel. No wonder the chief priests want Lazarus dead too (v. 10)—his very life proves Jesus' claims.[2]

Like Lazarus, our lives speak the gospel to others. For good or for bad, we influence those around us every day. Are we drawing them to Christ? Or are we pushing them away?

B. Five days before (vv. 12–19). Abruptly we are transported from the sleepy village of Bethany to the bustling metropolis of Jerusalem. With Passover just five days away, the city is bursting with people who have come to celebrate. Most of them had either witnessed Jesus bringing Lazarus out of the tomb or had at least heard about it. Now this miracle worker is coming to their city!

When they heard that Jesus was coming to Jerusalem, [they] took the branches of the palm trees, and went out to meet Him, and began to cry out, "Hosanna![3] Blessed is He who comes in the name of the Lord, even the King of Israel." And Jesus, finding a young donkey, sat on it; as it is written, "Fear not, daughter of Zion; behold, your King is coming, seated on a donkey's colt." (vv. 12b–15)

The Pharisees can't believe their eyes. They have always taught that the Messiah would come down from heaven on a white charger, taking command of the kingdom of Israel. But the people are paying royal homage to a local man riding into town on a dull-gray donkey.

---

2. All the priests were Sadducees, who did not believe in the resurrection of the dead.

3. Translated from the Hebrew and Greek, *hōsanna* means "save, we pray" or "save, now."

The Pharisees therefore said to one another, "You see that you are not doing any good; look, the world has gone after Him." (v. 19)

Blaming each other, they realize they've lost their grip on the people's hearts.

C. **Four days before** (vv. 20–50). Again John changes the scene without warning, introducing a third set of characters.

> Now there were certain Greeks among those who were going up to worship at the feast; these therefore came to Philip, who was from Bethsaida of Galilee, and began to ask him, saying, "Sir, we wish to see Jesus." (vv. 20–21)

The Greeks were wanderers, inquisitive nomads who scratched their names in the rocks of every city they visited. This tourist group has arrived in Jerusalem at the height of Passover, to the disgust of the Jews, who do not appreciate sharing their ethnic holiday with inconsiderate foreigners. Because Philip has a Greek name, perhaps this group thinks he will be sympathetic to their request. Unsure of what to do, Philip goes to Andrew, and together they bring the request to Jesus[4] (v. 22).

> And Jesus answered them, saying, "The hour has come for the Son of Man to be glorified." (v. 23)

Jesus responds as though the Greeks aren't even present. His mind is preoccupied with one thing—His death. From verse 23 through the end of the chapter, Jesus presents His last public teaching, concentrating on four major themes. First, the cross is imminent, only four days away (vv. 23, 27, 32). Second, the pain is great (v. 27). Third, the need is urgent (vv. 35–36). Fourth, the response will be varied—some will accept Him, while others will reject Him (vv. 37, 42, 43). Throughout this passage we see continual reminders of the closeness between Father and Son. Jesus anguishes over the cross, and His anguish is real, but an abiding peace overcomes the pain. He has accepted His Father's sovereign plan, which was designed before the creation of the world.

> "For I did not speak on My own initiative, but the Father Himself who sent Me has given Me commandment, what to say, and what to speak. And I know that His commandment is eternal life; therefore the things I speak, I speak just as the Father has told Me." (vv. 49–50)

---

4. Andrew is mentioned three times in the Bible, and each time he is bringing someone to Christ (see John 1:40–42, 6:8–9).

III. A Summary of the Truth

We can glean three principles from our study of these last days in Jesus' life.

A. Salvation is not limited to certain types. Remember Judas? He was Christ's disciple, the trusted treasurer. But he defected. Mary was emotional and unconventional, yet she embraced Christ with all her heart. Likewise, the Jews in the street believed Him, the Greek tourists were in awe of Him, but the religious officials rejected Him.

B. Worship is not limited to specific times. We can worship God anywhere and at any time. Mary worshiped at the dinner table. The crowd worshiped in the street. The Greeks worshiped as He spoke. There is no limit to when we can worship, and sometimes our most meaningful worship times are spontaneous.

C. Christianity is not lived on selfish terms. The Christian life is a paradox: to keep, we must give ... to be great, we must serve ... to live, we must die. And not until we die will we realize the real joy of giving, or the emptiness of keeping.

Living Insights

Study One

As we studied John 12, we saw the beginning of Christ's last week on earth. John devoted ten chapters to this last week, and the other Gospel writers recorded it at length in their accounts as well, underscoring the importance of what He said and did during this time.

- To get a better handle on the events in Christ's final week, let's invest our time today in reading the accounts in the other three Gospels. Read Matthew 21–28, Mark 11–16, and Luke 19–24. No need for charts or notes—just read and reflect.

🐴 *Living Insights*

We cannot ignore a question brought up in this study: If you knew you had only one more week to live, what would you do? It's a question worth considering.

● Using the space below, put your thoughts in writing.

_____

_____

_____

_____

_____

_____

_____

_____

_____

_____

_____

_____

_____

_____

_____

_____

_____

_____

_____

_____

_____

Humility Personified
John 13:1–17

Humility. Confucius called it "the solid foundation of all the virtues."[1] The Greek word means "low" or "to stoop low," and it carries the idea of serving another person. That is clearly the usage in Matthew 11:28–29.

> "Come to Me, all who are weary and heavy-laden, and I will give you rest. Take My yoke upon you, and learn from Me, for I am gentle and humble in heart; and You shall find rest for your souls."

It is Christ's example of humility that Paul appeals to in his exhortation to serve one another.

> Do nothing from selfishness or empty conceit, but with humility of mind let each of you regard one another as more important than himself; do not merely look out for your own personal interests, but also for the interests of others. Have this attitude in yourselves which was also in Christ Jesus, who, although He existed in the form of God, did not regard equality with God a thing to be grasped, but emptied Himself, taking the form of a bond-servant, and being made in the likeness of men. And being found in appearance as a man, He humbled Himself by becoming obedient to the point of death, even death on a cross. (Phil. 2:3–8)

In the shadow of that cross, Jesus spent His last night and last meal with the disciples. There we see Him, not seated at the place of honor, but assuming the lowly position of a servant. And there we see Him exemplifying servanthood to the disciples—by washing their feet.

I. Background and Setting

The location for the Last Supper is Jerusalem; the occasion, the night before the Jewish Feast of the Passover.

> Now before the Feast of the Passover, Jesus knowing that His hour had come that He should depart out of this world to the Father, having loved His own who were in the world, He loved them to the end. (John 13:1–2)

Just before His first miracle, Jesus told His mother that His hour had not yet come (2:4). Now that hour is fast approaching. His life and ministry are winding down to an eleventh-hour climax, and all heaven will stop for the tolling of that mournful bell. Yet, this hour doesn't creep up on Christ and overtake Him unaware, although His

---

1. As quoted in *Five Thousand Quotations for All Occasions,* ed. Lewis C. Henry (Garden City, N.Y.: Doubleday and Co., 1945), p. 126.

64

eyes never stray to the clock to watch the seconds of His life tick away. Our passage indicates that He knows His time has come (v. 1). He knows He has less than fifteen hours to live. But His brow is not knit in anxiety. His eyes do not dart nervously back and forth for a way of escape. He knows death is His destiny. He knows that not only is His *death* the Father's will (Isa. 53:10), but even His *betrayal* (compare Luke 22:22).

> Jesus [knew] that the Father had given all things into His hands, and that He had come forth from God, and was going back to God. (v. 3)

II. Illustrating Humility

As time moves forward in dicing and deliberate steps, Christ's every word is weighed; every movement, measured.

> [Jesus] rose from supper, and laid aside His garments; and taking a towel, He girded Himself about. Then He poured water into the basin, and began to wash the disciples' feet, and to wipe them with the towel with which He was girded. (vv. 4–5)

A. Reasons. There are at least two reasons why Jesus chooses this activity on His last night with His disciples.

1. **Their hearts are proud.** Christ gathered His friends to tell them of His impending suffering and betrayal (Luke 22:15, 21–22); but in the midst of His discussion the disciples get into a petty argument about rank...an ongoing dispute they have pursued all too often (see 9:46).

   > And they began to discuss among themselves which one of them it might be who was going to do this thing. And there arose also a dispute among them as to which one of them was regarded to be greatest. (22:23–24)

2. **Their feet are dirty.** As Jesus' troubled eyes fall on the disciples' tired and travel-worn feet, He seizes the opportunity both to end the argument and to instruct them in a lesson they will never forget—a lesson that touches not only their feet but their hearts as well.

   > The roads of Palestine were quite unsurfaced and uncleaned. In dry weather they were inches deep in dust, and in wet weather they were liquid mud. The shoes the ordinary people wore were sandals; and these sandals were simply soles held on to the foot by a few straps. They gave little protection against the dust or the mud of the roads. For that reason there were always great waterpots at the door of the house; and a servant

was there with a ewer and a towel to wash the soiled feet of the guests as they came in.[2] But no servants grace this austere banquet. And no one in this crowd stoops to wash anyone's feet. The disciples are ready to fight for a throne, but not for a towel. So Jesus assumes the role, demonstrating that He did "not come to be served, but to serve" (Matt. 20:28).

B. Principles. In verses 4–12, four principles emerge regarding humility.

    1. Humility is unannounced. Jesus does not say: "OK, men, I'm now going to demonstrate humility!" On the contrary, Jesus abhors such obvious self-exaltation, as His teaching concerning the scribes and Pharisees indicates:

> "And they love the place of honor at banquets, and the chief seats in the synagogues, and respectful greetings in the market places, and being called by men, Rabbi. But do not be called Rabbi; for One is your Teacher, and you are all brothers. And do not call anyone on earth your father; for One is your Father, He who is in heaven. And do not be called leaders; for one is your Leader, that is, Christ. But the greatest among you shall be your servant. And whoever exalts himself shall be humbled; and whoever humbles himself shall be exalted." (Matt. 23:6–12)

No, greatness does not consist of exaltation but abasement (Phil. 2:8–9, 1 Pet. 5:5–6). As nature teaches us, the branch most full of fruit bends the lowest. Turning back to John 13, we'll see what at first glance appears to be humility. But we find that, in reality, it is only a thin veil concealing Peter's pride.

> Then He poured water into the basin, and began to wash the disciples' feet, and to wipe them with the towel with which He was girded. And so He came to Simon Peter. He said to Him, "Lord, do You wash my feet?" Jesus answered and said to him, "What I do you do not realize now, but you shall understand hereafter." (vv. 5–7)

Embarrassed to admit his need, Peter is resistant and unwilling to submit.

---

2. William Barclay, *The Gospel of John,* vol. 2, The Daily Study Bible Series (Edinburgh, Scotland: Saint Andrew Press, 1956), p. 161.

2. **Humility is willing to receive—without embarrassment.** Tucking his feet under himself, Peter pulls away. Jesus stoops, but Peter resists . . . a resistance that leads to rebuke.

> Peter said to Him, "Never shall You wash my feet!" Jesus answered him, "If I do not wash you, you have no part with Me." (v. 8)

3. **Humility is not a sign of weakness.** Although performing a subservient task, Jesus can boldly assert: "Peter, you're in error!" In response, Peter swings to the other side of the pendulum.

> Simon Peter said to Him, "Lord, not my feet only, but also my hands and my head." (v. 9)

With discernment and strength, Jesus puts His finger on the pulse of a critical theological matter.

> "He who has bathed needs only to wash his feet, but is completely clean; and you are clean, but not all of you." (v. 10)

John helps us see the subtle yet significant distinction through the use of two different Greek terms, one meaning "bathed," the other meaning "wash" or "sponge." The idea is this: *once bathed, always bathed.* Customarily, people bathed in the privacy of their homes before attending a dinner engagement. But their feet would get dirty walking through the dusty streets to the host's home. When they arrived, what they needed was not a bath, but only a sponging off of their feet. Spiritually, God bathes us at conversion, cleansing our scarlet sins white as snow. But walking through life's dirty streets, we pick up some of the world's grunge and grime. What we need in that case is not another bath—just cleansing. As 1 John 1:9 states:

> If we confess our sins, He is faithful and righteous to forgive us our sins and to cleanse us from all unrighteousness.

Returning to John 13, we see a parenthetical clarification of Jesus' comment at the end of verse 10.

> For He knew the one who was betraying Him; for this reason He said, "Not all of you are clean." (v. 11)

4. **Humility does not play favorites.** It is neither selective nor exclusive. Jesus washes each foot—even Judas's. If Jesus were only human, He probably would have been tempted to use boiling water to wash Peter's feet and ice-cold water to wash Judas's. But He didn't come to scold or to shun; He came to serve . . . gently and humbly.

III. Discussing Humility

When Jesus finishes, He reclines at the table (v. 12), and a hush settles over the room. All are looking down at their cleansed and refreshed feet, suddenly self-conscious in their shame. In perfect pedagogical fashion, Jesus draws them in with an approach that drives His point into their hearts.

A. The approach. With a penetrating question, Jesus makes sure His message is clearly understood.

"Do you know what I have done to you? You call Me Teacher and Lord; and you are right, for so I am. If I then, the Lord and the Teacher, washed your feet, you also ought to wash one another's feet. For I gave you an example that you also should do as I did to you. Truly, truly, I say to you, a slave is not greater than his master; neither is one who is sent greater than the one who sent him. If you know these things, you are blessed if you do them." (vv. 12b–17)

B. The application. Two lessons emerge from this example. One, humility includes serving one another, not just the Lord. Two, happiness results from demonstrating humility, not just learning about it.

A Concluding Thought about Our God

Who is like the Lord our God,
Who is enthroned on high,
Who humbles Himself to behold
The things that are in heaven and in the earth?
He raises the poor from the dust,
And lifts the needy from the ash heap,
To make them sit with princes,
With the princes of His people. (Ps. 113:5–8)

🕮 Living Insights

Study One ▬▬▬

The key to understanding John 13 is found in verse 15: "For I gave you an example that you also should do as I did to you." Let's pursue a fuller understanding of these verses.

- Reread John 13:1–17. Look for words you consider important, and jot them down in the space provided. Use the other blanks to give the meanings of the words and to make a statement about the significance of each word.

John 13:1–17

Key Word: _____ Meaning: _____

Significance: _____

Key Word: _____ Meaning: _____

Significance: _____

Key Word: _____ Meaning: _____

Significance: _____

Key Word: _____ Meaning: _____

Significance: _____

Key Word: _____ Meaning: _____

Significance: _____

Key Word: _____ Meaning: _____

Significance: _____

Continued on next page

69

Key Word: _____ Meaning: _____

_____

Significance: _____

_____

Key Word: _____ Meaning: _____

_____

Significance: _____

_____

Key Word: _____ Meaning: _____

_____

Significance: _____

_____

Key Word: _____ Meaning: _____

_____

Significance: _____

_____

Living Insights

Study Two ▬▬▬▬▬▬▬▬▬▬▬▬▬▬▬▬▬▬▬▬▬▬▬▬▬▬▬▬

Humility comes from serving one another, not just Christ. Happiness comes from demonstrating humility, not just learning about it. With applications like these, we need to get busy!

- What can you do to demonstrate true humility this week? Is there someone to whom you can offer the kind of service Christ offered His disciples in this passage? Think of something specific and tangible that you can do in the next few days. Start thinking in terms of serving Christ through serving people. It will be exciting to see how God will provide opportunities for you to "wash feet" this week!

How High Is Your A.Q.?

John 13:18–30

Leonardo da Vinci's timeless masterpiece, *Last Supper*, captures the dramatic moment when Jesus announces to His disciples that one of them will betray Him.

Turmoil disrupts the Passover table as the twelve disciples react to Christ's forewarning. In capturing this moment before the traitor is revealed, Leonardo plumbed a psychological depth unknown in previous paintings of the Last Supper.[1]

In the painting, the disciples are grouped in threes, artistically heightening the drama. And in each cluster of three, all the participants are aghast with shock, expressing amazement to one another. All, that is, except Judas.

Recoiling from Jesus' words, Judas clutches a leather pouch . . . the pouch that holds his betrayal fee. Da Vinci ironically depicts him knocking over the salt cellar. One of the men chosen to be the salt of the world is the very one about to rub salt into the Savior's wounds.

In the shadow of his own guilt, Judas clutches more than thirty pieces of silver. He holds tightly in his heart a secret only he and Jesus share at that table: he is the betrayer.

I. Definition of A.Q.

The story of Judas and the Last Supper shows us something magnificent about the Savior and about His ability to accept others in spite of the sin that clings to them. As an I.Q. test measures our minds, indicating our intelligence quotient, an A.Q. test measures our attitudes, indicating our acceptance quotient. In our lesson today, we'll take a look at the A.Q. of Jesus with regard to Judas, and then we'll turn the test on our own lives.

A. Meaning. Our acceptance quotient is our ability to receive another person without inner restrictions of prejudice or outer requirements of performance.

B. Clarification. Our acceptance quotient does not nullify discernment; nor does it deny depravity. But it does allow for maximum freedom and individuality. There are few examples better than the Last Supper to help guide our thoughts along these lines. In John 13:18–30, we find two individuals face-to-face who could not have been more different: Jesus and Judas; the former with an A.Q. of ten, the latter with an A.Q. of zero.

---

1. Carlo Bertelli, "Restoration Reveals the Last Supper," *National Geographic* 164 (November 1983), p. 668.

II. Illustration of A.Q.

Just as the name Benedict Arnold has become synonymous with betrayal in American history, so the name Judas is linked with treason in biblical history.

A. Truth about the traitor. Judas was a hypocrite. With his polished exterior, he looked every inch a disciple; within, however, he was a traitor to the core. Looking back on this night years later, John is quick to point an indicting finger in Judas's direction (see v. 2). But at the time, only Jesus knew of the disciple's plot to betray Him (see v. 11). Christ's knowledge of the betrayal was not some sudden piece of information that surfaced at the dinner table; it had been revealed a thousand years earlier in the Psalms.

> "I do not speak of all of you. I know the ones I have chosen; but it is that the Scripture may be fulfilled, 'He who eats my bread has lifted up his heel against Me.' " (v. 18)[2]

B. Treatment of the traitor. Verses 21–22 are the verses that inspired da Vinci to paint the *Last Supper,* a fresco in the monastery of Santa Maria delle Grazie in Milan, Italy.

> When Jesus had said this, He became troubled in spirit, and testified, and said, "Truly, truly, I say to you, that one of you will betray Me."

The seating arrangement, however, was not quite as da Vinci presents it, as verses 23–26 indicate.

> There was reclining on Jesus' breast one of His disciples, whom Jesus loved. Simon Peter therefore gestured to him, and said to him, "Tell us who it is of whom He is speaking." He, leaning back thus on Jesus' breast, said to Him, "Lord, who is it?" Jesus therefore answered, "That is the one for whom I shall dip the morsel and give it to him." So when He had dipped the morsel, He took and gave it to Judas, the son of Simon Iscariot.

First of all, the Jews did not sit at traditional tables as we know them. Their tables were low, solid blocks with pillows or pallets around them for the guests to recline upon (see v. 23a). They reclined, leaning on the left elbow, leaving the right hand free to eat with. Sitting in such a way, a man's head was quite literally in the breast of the person who was reclining to his left. That

---

2. The passage quoted is Psalm 41:9. The eating of bread together symbolizes close fellowship. Most commentators interpret "lifted up his heel" as a metaphor derived from the image of a horse's hoof preparing to kick, indicating a hurtful or destructive act.

would place John, the author of the gospel, on Jesus' right (see v. 23b). Since it is obvious that Jesus also spoke privately with Judas (see vv. 26–27), most likely that disciple was seated at the left of Jesus.

And the revealing thing about that is that the place on the left of the host was the place of highest honour, kept for the most intimate friend. When that meal began, Jesus must have said to Judas: "Judas, come and sit beside me to-night; I want specially to talk to you." The very inviting of Judas to that seat was an appeal.[3]

C. **Change in the traitor.** Realizing the power of Jesus' love to soften the heart of even the most mercenary of traitors, Satan steps in to make sure that nothing foils his assassination plot.

And after the morsel, Satan then entered into him. Jesus therefore said to him, "What you do, do quickly." Now no one of those reclining at the table knew for what purpose He had said this to him. For some were supposing, because Judas had the money box, that Jesus was saying to him, "Buy the things we have need of for the feast"; or else, that he should give something to the poor. (vv. 27–29)

The Limits of Acceptance

Remember: acceptance doesn't mean putting a blind-fold on discernment or ignoring depravity.

Scripture clearly states that there are times when we are *not* to fellowship with certain people. John implores us, in his second epistle, not to commune closely with anyone involved in false cults. In his third epistle he declares that the church cannot tolerate Diotrephes, an errant, self-willed brother. And in 1 Corinthians 5:9–12, Paul clearly teaches us to not only separate ourselves from an immoral believer but actually remove that person from the church (see also 2 Thess. 3:6, 14–15).

There is a time to accept fellowship and a time to reject it. Jesus held out His hand to Judas until he consciously decided to carry out his plan. And we, too, must hold out our hand of fellowship until a person takes that rebellious step outside the doctrinal and moral circle that encloses us.

---

3. William Barclay, *The Gospel of John*, vol. 2, The Daily Study Bible Series (Edinburgh, Scotland: Saint Andrew Press, 1956), p. 169.

D. Reaction of the traitor. Like Pharaoh, unbending and unchanged, Judas' heart remains hardened. And so he ventures out into the cold, dark alleyways of betrayal—far from the Light that loved him and offered him warmth.

> And so after receiving the morsel he went out immediately; and it was night. (v. 30)

III. Application of A.Q.

Using this passage as a practical basis of comparison, we want to drive home the importance of a high A.Q. score in three areas.

A. Willingness to accept people without partiality. The subject is prejudice. Look at James 2:1–4.

> My brethren, do not hold your faith in our glorious Lord Jesus Christ with an attitude of personal favoritism. For if a man comes into your assembly with a gold ring and dressed in fine clothes, and there also comes in a poor man in dirty clothes, and you pay special attention to the one who is wearing the fine clothes, and say, "You sit here in a good place," and you say to the poor man, "You stand over there, or sit down by my footstool," have you not made distinctions among yourselves, and become judges with evil motives?

The root of preferring one person over another is sin, as James points out later in chapter 2.

> But if you show partiality, you are committing sin and are convicted by the law as transgressors. (v. 9)

How do you respond when somebody who doesn't quite fit the typical membership profile comes to your church? Say the person is poor, with threadbare, unwashed clothes. Or maybe the haircut doesn't make quite the proper doctrinal statement. What if the person is mentally, physically, or emotionally handicapped? Or divorced? Or the wrong color . . . or of a different political persuasion?

B. Willingness to accept another style without jealousy or criticism. No one exemplified this more than Jesus.

> John said to Him, "Teacher, we saw someone casting out demons in Your name, and we tried to hinder him because he was not following us." But Jesus said, "Do not hinder him, for there is no one who shall perform a miracle in My name, and be able soon afterward to speak evil of Me. For he who is not against us is for us." (Mark 9:38–40)

This same emphasis can be seen in Paul's life, whose major concern was to reach the world with the message of the gospel.

How the world was reached was of significantly lesser concern (Phil. 1:15–18). Does a pride of style or size characterize your evaluation of churches? Does a pride of philosophy or personality keep you from accepting another church's contribution to the spread of the gospel? Certainly John the Baptist, with his unusual garb and hermit's ways, doesn't fit our mold of evangelist. Yet God used him as the forerunner to His Son.

C. **Willingness to accept offenses without holding a grudge.** Remember, Jesus washed the very heels that were raised against Him … and fed a morsel to the very lips that would kiss His cheek to identify Him to His captors. Emulating the example of Christ, Paul exhorts us in Romans 12:14–21.

> Bless those who persecute you; bless and curse not. Rejoice with those who rejoice, and weep with those who weep. Be of the same mind toward one another; do not be haughty in mind, but associate with the lowly. Do not be wise in your own estimation. Never pay back evil for evil to anyone. Respect what is right in the sight of all men. If possible, so far as it depends on you, be at peace with all men. Never take your own revenge, beloved, but leave room for the wrath of God, for it is written, "Vengeance is Mine, I will repay," says the Lord. "But if your enemy is hungry, feed him, and if he is thirsty, give him a drink; for in so doing you will heap burning coals upon his head." Do not be overcome by evil, but overcome evil with good.

Do you plot how to get even when wronged, or do you truly forgive and forget? Do you look for opportunities to gossip about someone who's offended you, or do you speak well of those who have wounded you with their words? Do you stomp off and leave the class or the church like a spoiled child, or do you stay and try to make peace?

The Fragrance of Forgiveness

It is said that forgiveness is the fragrance the violet sheds on the heel that has crushed it. If so, could there be a fragrance as sweet in all the Bible as that of Jesus washing the feet of the very one whose heel was raised against Him?

Many things have been said against Christ, but He has never been accused of not practicing what He preached. And Jesus' last moments with His betrayer are a perfect example of His exhortation to "love your enemies, and

---

pray for those who persecute you" (Matt. 5:44). This He did even to the end, when He hung on that shameful cross and prayed: "Father, forgive them; for they do not know what they are doing" (Luke 23:34).

How do you respond when a heel of betrayal comes crushing down on you? No one relishes being stepped on, any more than a violet does. But when it happens, let the example of Jesus guide your response. Let His fragrance exude in you a potent forgiveness, reaching the nostrils of the one whose heel has hurt you.

Living Insights

Study One

In order to work on your acceptance quotient, it's important to know the elements of biblical acceptance. In his letter to the Romans, the apostle Paul gives us some valuable insights into this issue.

- Turn in your New Testament to Romans 14 and 15. As you read these two chapters, see if you can discover elements of acceptance. Write them in the chart that follows.

Elements of Biblical Acceptance—Romans 14–15	
Verses	Elements

Verses	Elements

 Living Insights

Study Two ━━━━━━━━━━━━━━━━━━━━━━━━━━━━

Now that you've identified the elements of biblical acceptance, it's time for you to take your own A.Q. test.

- Rate yourself in the following three areas, with 10 being highest.

  1. How willing am I to accept people without partiality?

     1   2   3   4   5   6   7   8   9   10

  2. How willing am I to accept another style without jealousy or criticism?

     1   2   3   4   5   6   7   8   9   10

  3. How willing am I to accept offenses without holding a grudge?

     1   2   3   4   5   6   7   8   9   10

- Now total up the three scores. How high is your A.Q.? What can you do to improve your score?

Agapē ... Authentic Love
John 13:31–38

In his book *The Mark of a Christian,* Dr. Francis Schaeffer discusses the quality that distinctively sets believers apart as children of God. It is not a pithy bumper sticker or an ichthus dangled pendulously from the neck or a gilded dove decorously impaled upon the lapel. These are only symbols of our faith. The true mark of the Christian is love.

Arthur Pink, in his commentary on John, says it well:

> Love is the *badge* of Christian discipleship. It is not knowledge, nor orthodoxy, nor fleshly activities, but (supremely) *love* which identifies a follower of the Lord Jesus. As the disciples of the Pharisees were known by their phylacteries, as the disciples of John were known by their baptism, and every school by its particular shibboleth, so the mark of a true Christian is *love;* and that, a genuine, active love, not in words but in deeds.[1]

In John 13, Jesus gives the disciples a mandate that adds a new dimension to the meaning of love. And this new dimension not only changes lives but, in a compelling way, shows the world that we belong to Jesus.

I. Jesus and the Disciples
In verses 31–35, Jesus discusses two main topics: His departure and His command to the disciples.

A. His departure. In our last lesson, we left the disciples gathered with Jesus at a final meal together. As soon as Judas leaves, Jesus speaks of another departure—His own.

When therefore he had gone out, Jesus said, "Now is the Son of Man glorified, and God is glorified in Him; if God is glorified in Him, God will also glorify Him in Himself, and will glorify Him immediately." (vv. 31–32)

Five times in this passage Jesus uses some form of the word *glorify.* For Him, death is not a mournful tragedy but a magnificent triumph. It is glorious, not gruesome. That is heaven's vantage point (compare Ps. 116:15). Jesus knows that His teaching is difficult for the disciples to understand, so He patiently assures them by tenderly expressing His paternal care for them.

"Little children, I am with you a little while longer. You shall seek Me; and as I said to the Jews, I now say

---

1. Arthur Pink, *Exposition of the Gospel of John,* vol. 1 (Grand Rapids, Mich.: Zondervan Publishing House, 1968), p. 341.

to you also, 'Where I am going, you cannot come.'"
(v. 33)[2]

Jesus shifts His tone in verse 33. He no longer speaks in mystical shades of meaning, but becomes very explicit. In doing so, He presents the puzzled disciples with three hard facts they would have to face: first, His departure is imminent; second, people will look for Him and be confused; and third, nobody can come with Him—including the eleven. There's a distinct finality in Jesus' words, which poses an enormous problem for the disciples: How will they go on? With their Master gone, what will be their identity? Won't they lose their impact?

B. His command. Anticipating their insecurity, Jesus stabilizes His disciples with a weighty command.

> "A new commandment I give to you, that you love one another, even as I have loved you, that you also love one another. By this all men will know that you are My disciples, if you have love for one another."
> (vv. 34–35)

In these verses Jesus not only commands a new dynamic, He predicts a new impact as well.

1. **The dynamic.** The first thing to note about Jesus' command is that He terms it "new." It is not simply additional or different, it is fresh and unique.

> Jesus is not speaking here of love to all men but of love within the brotherhood. Love itself is not a new commandment, but an old one (Lev. 19:18). The new thing appears to be the mutual affection that Christians have for one another on account of Christ's great love for them. . . . Jesus Himself has set the example. He calls on them now to follow in His steps.[3]

The word Jesus uses in verse 35 is *agapē*. Of the Greeks' four words for love, this one is the capstone. Essentially, it means to seek the highest good of another.[4] This type of love refuses to respond negatively, refuses to reject, refuses to demand conditions, and refuses to nitpick the lint off someone's soul. When Jesus says "as I have loved you," He

---

2. "Little children" is a term expressing affection that is found only once in this Gospel. Other than in this reference, the phrase is seen only seven times, all in 1 John.

3. Leon Morris, *The Gospel According to John* (Grand Rapids, Mich.: William B. Eerdmans Publishing Co., 1971), p. 633.

4. For a more detailed analysis of agapē love, see 1 Corinthians 13:4–8a. For an example of this love, see Philippians 2:3–8.

sets Himself up as the standard by which they are to forever measure their love for one another. He is telling them, "I left the splendors and comforts of Heaven because I loved you. I called you to be Mine, knowing full well your faults. I taught you, even when you were stubborn and closed-minded. I corrected you when you stepped out of line. I washed your feet on the way to My death. All this was for your highest good. My interest was not in Myself, but in you."

2. **The impact.** In a word: incredible. It extends to all men (v. 35). Nobody can ignore authentic love. Nothing is more impressive than unselfish attention. The word *know* in verse 35 does not refer to theoretical knowledge but to knowledge gained by first-hand, rub-of-the-shoulders observation. And what will these observers know? That we belong to Jesus! Our love for each other will be a distinctive badge of His ownership. An ichthus links us to a belief . . . a cross links us to a religion . . . but love links us to Jesus Himself. That's the mark that matters—the mark that makes a difference.

┌─ *A Quote to Consider* ─────────────────────────────
│   "It is probably impossible to love any human being
│   simply 'too much.' We may love him too much *in pro-*
│   *portion* to our love for God; but it is the smallness of
│   our love for God, not the greatness of our love for the
│   man, that constitutes the inordinacy."[5]

II. Jesus and Simon Peter

Apparently, Christ's words about His departure hit Peter like a two-by-four, because he completely misses the new commandment.

A. Destiny questioned. Look closely at Peter's remark.

Simon Peter said to Him, "Lord, where are You going?" Jesus answered, "Where I go, you cannot follow Me now; but you shall follow later." Peter said to Him, "Lord, why can I not follow You right now?" (vv. 36–37a)

It is obvious from his remarks that Peter is interested not only in Jesus' leaving but also in his being left behind.

B. Loyalty declared. In an impulsive but improvident expression of sincerity, Peter declares his undying allegiance to Jesus. "I will lay down my life for You." (v. 37b)

---

5. C. S. Lewis, *The Four Loves* (New York, N.Y.: Harcourt Brace Jovanovich, 1960), p. 170.

C. **Reality predicted.** With the sharp edge of reality, Jesus lightly touches the surface of Peter's loyalty—a touch that draws blood. Jesus answered, "Will you lay down your life for Me? Truly, truly, I say to you, a cock shall not crow, until you deny Me three times." (v. 38)

III. Jesus and You

From this passage emerge three truths about how your love should be expressed to other Christians.

A. **Authentic love is unconditional in its expression.** There are no *ifs* attached to authentic love . . . no threats . . . no demands. Do you exhibit this type of love to your mate? How about to your children? Or do you withhold your love until they've lived up to your standards? Do they feel unconditionally loved, or do they feel they're constantly trying to gain your acceptance?

B. **Authentic love is unselfish in its motive.** Remember Paul's words: Love "is not jealous . . . does not seek its own" (1 Cor. 13:4–5). Love does not manipulate to get its way. Love always looks after number two—not exclusively after number one (see Phil. 2:3–4). How about you? When you show love to someone else, is it weighed in the balance of what you will receive in return? True love gives—with no thought of getting anything in return.

C. **Authentic love is unlimited in its benefits.** When you love unconditionally and unselfishly, you always walk away the winner. Not only are others built up and encouraged, but so are you! Of course, when you love this way, you become vulnerable. But if you never step out on a limb with people, you'll never grasp the fruit of nourishing relationships.

A Final Thought

"To love at all is to be vulnerable. Love anything, and your heart will certainly be wrung and possibly be broken. If you want to make sure of keeping it intact, you must give your heart to no one, not even to an animal. Wrap it carefully round with hobbies and little luxuries; avoid all entanglements; lock it up safe in the casket or coffin of your selfishness. But in that casket—safe, dark, motionless, airless—it will change. It will not be broken; it will become unbreakable, impenetrable, irredeemable."[6]

---

6. Lewis, *The Four Loves*, p. 169.

81

Living Insights

Have you ever tried to express your love on paper? Love has prompted more songs, poems, films, books, and speeches than any other subject. Yet the finest words of love are found in God's love letter, the Bible.

● Earlier in this study guide we introduced paraphrasing. Let's return to that exercise and apply it to the thirteenth chapter of John's Gospel. Remember, paraphrasing is writing out the text in your own words. It allows you to enhance your study by expanding on the meanings and emotions represented in the passage. Pick out your favorite verses in the passage and paraphrase them in the following space.

My Favorite Verses from John 13

_____

_____

_____

_____

_____

_____

_____

_____

_____

_____

_____

_____

_____

_____

_____

_____

_____

_____

_____

_____

_____

_____

_____

_____

_____

_____

_____

_____

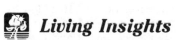 *Living Insights*

Study Two ▬▬▬▬▬▬▬▬▬▬▬▬▬▬▬▬▬▬▬▬▬

After studying John 13, you should understand what authentic agapē love is. Now it's your turn to express yourself!

● Today, write a love letter to someone. It may be someone you haven't seen in a long time, or it may be someone that lives in the same house with you. It may be someone with whom you communicate every day or someone you haven't talked to in months. This task is a labor of love. Tell this person how you feel and how much he or she means to you. Try to avoid clichés and well-worn phrases—be innovative. And be sure to mail it!

Tranquil Words for Troubled Hearts
John 14:1-24

For the prodigal son, who left his family and squandered his inheritance in indulgent, immoral living, home was a faraway place. Yet thoughts of home tugged at his heart like a magnet to steel and brought him to his senses. Returning home, he found embracing arms, robes and rings, fatted calves, music and dancing. There he found acceptance, restoration, fellowship, and joy. There he found a tranquil haven for his troubled heart.

Our homes are designed to be a hint of heaven, the dim glimmer of a more beautiful, more secure, more peaceful place. J. Howard Payne wrote fondly of this in the poem "Home Sweet Home."

> 'Mid pleasures and palaces though
>   we may roam,
> Be it ever so humble, there's no place
>   like Home.[1]

Payne's words conjur up images of the 1939 movie *The Wizard of Oz,* where Dorothy awakes from her harrowing adventures in the fantasy world of Oz, repeating over and over: "There's no place like home." Troubled by her dream, Dorothy takes comfort in being home—safe in her own bed, cuddled by her own blanket, surrounded by her own family and friends. Kansas and Auntie Em never looked so good!

For Christians, our pilgrimage here on earth is like Dorothy's journey down the Yellow Brick Road. It is filled with illusory dreams, frightening experiences, and disappointing realities, in spite of our hopes. And the farther we travel down that road, the more our intuitive self insists that this is not our home, heaven is.

In John 14, Jesus senses the troubled hearts within His disciples and calms them with tranquil words—words that turn their thoughts toward home.

I. Thoughts That Trouble the Heart
The chapter break between John 13:38, where we ended the last lesson, and 14:1, where we start today's study, is abrupt and unfortunate because it leaves us without sufficient background to the passage. Contextually, the words of Jesus in chapter 14 answer Peter's question in 13:36–37 which, in turn, refers back to Jesus' statement about His departure in verse 33. This explains why the disciples

---

1. As quoted in *Five Thousand Quotations for All Occasions,* ed. Lewis C. Henry (Garden City, N.Y.: Doubleday and Co., 1945), p. 123.

are troubled (14:1, 27). Let's take a closer look at the thoughts that have troubled not only *their* hearts but *ours* as well.

A. Thoughts regarding death. Jesus had told the disciples He would die soon (13:33a), causing them to be afraid. The fear of death, either our own or a loved one's, troubles our lives like a hurricane sweeping over a serene harbor. And, anchored in the shallows, our little boats of faith are easily dashed against the rocks by fear's fury.

B. Thoughts regarding trials. Jesus then told His disciples that they could not come with Him when He would leave (v. 33b). This confusing trial made them anxious and frustrated. For us, daily living takes its toll. We tear our hair out or bite our nails to the nub over the day-to-day tempests that blow through our lives. But for all our worry, we are left with only a handful of hair where there could have been character and ten throbbing fingers where there could have been faith.

C. Thoughts regarding disloyalty. Upon hearing Peter's strong pledge of loyalty (vv. 36–37), Jesus predicted the disciple's impending denial (v. 38). Disobedience and disloyalty always produce guilt. Like Peter, all of us have denied Christ in some way or another. If we haven't denied Him with words, then we have in deeds. And if not in deeds, then certainly in thoughts.

II. Truths That Quiet the Heart

The first twenty verses of chapter 14 link together a chain of counsel so strong and secure that it will help us weather even the most inclement of circumstances.

A. Personal faith in a personal God brings personal strength.

> "Let not your heart be troubled; believe in God, believe also in Me." (v. 1)

The verbs are present imperatives, with the sense of: "Keep on believing in God . . . keep on believing in Me." The disciples had trusted Jesus to put them in the boat of salvation; now they must trust Him to bring them through the storm and safely to harbor. Every test that blows our way can either fill our sails with faith or break our mast from the strain of unbelief.

B. While preparing a place for us, Christ is preparing us for that place.

> "In My Father's house are many dwelling places;[2] if it were not so, I would have told you; for I go to prepare

2. "The Greek word is *monē,* which comes from the verb *menō,* 'remain' or 'dwell.' The noun occurs (in NT) only here and in verse 23. . . . The rendering 'mansions' in verse 2 comes from

Footnote continued on next page

85

a place for you. And if I go and prepare a place for you, I will come again, and receive you to Myself; that where I am, there you may be also." (vv. 2–3)

As God fashions us for heaven, the tools He uses most often are trials and troubles (Rom. 5:3–4; compare Eph. 2:10, Phil. 2:13). Pressures are part of the process of making us perfect and complete, as James informs us.

Consider it all joy, my brethren, when you encounter various trials, knowing that the testing of your faith produces endurance. And let endurance have its perfect result, that you may be perfect and complete, lacking in nothing. (1:2–4)

Jesus' claim in John 14:4 prompts a question from the empirical mind of Thomas: "How do we know the way [to your Father's house]?" (v. 5). To which Jesus answers:

"I am the way, and the truth, and the life; no one comes to the Father, but through Me." (v. 6)

The Living Way

Imagine yourself asking for directions in a strange town. Suppose the other person says: "Take the first left here and go left at the second intersection. Turn right at the second street and go left when it makes a Y, and then go right." Chances are you'll get lost halfway there.

But suppose that person says: "Follow me. I'll take you there." In that case, the person *is* the way. And that's precisely the case with Jesus. He doesn't point the way in the distance or draw us some impersonal map. He takes us by the hand and leads us. If you're lost, or if you've played the prodigal and simply strayed, Jesus is the way home to the Father—the *only* way. Won't you place your hand in His and let Him lead you there?

C. **The sovereign hand of God is at work.** As Job says: "He knows the way I take; / When He has tried me, I shall come forth as gold" (23:10). That was true in Job's life, and it was also true in Christ's: "the Father abiding in Me does *His* works" (John 14:10b, emphasis added). Jesus declared that the Father was sovereignly involved in His works. And that included troubles. We know God is involved in the refining process. The question is, How pure is the gold coming out of His furnace?

the Latin Vulgate *mansiones*. The correct rendering of *monai* is 'dwelling places' (NASB) or 'rooms.' " Ralph Earle, *Word Meanings in the New Testament* (Grand Rapids, Mich.: Baker Book House, 1986), p. 92.

D. Greater things occur when we pray in Jesus' name, that the Father may be glorified.

"Truly, truly, I say to you, he who believes in Me, the works that I do shall he do also; and greater works than these shall he do; because I go to the Father. And whatever you ask in My name, that will I do, that the Father may be glorified in the Son. If you ask Me anything in My name, I will do it." (vv. 12–14)

Like Aladdin's lamp, these verses have suffered centuries of misuse. All too often, Christ has been looked on as a magic genie; and prayer, the fervent rub to the lamp. So many times, our prayers are like a stanza from "Old MacDonald's Farm": "a gimme gimme here and a gimme gimme there . . . here a gimme . . . there a gimme . . . everywhere a gimme gimme." But the verse is not a carte blanche to gratify our every desire. Notice that our preface to prayer should be "in My name" and our purpose for prayer is "that the Father may be glorified in the Son" (v. 13).

E. You are not alone; you have an inward Helper. For the first time, Jesus informs His troubled disciples about the Holy Spirit.

"And I will ask the Father, and He will give you another Helper,[3] that He may be with you forever; that is the Spirit of truth, whom the world cannot receive, because it does not behold Him or know Him, but you know Him because He abides with you, and will be in you. I will not leave you as orphans; I will come to you." (vv. 16–18)

In verse 16, the term *another* means literally, "another of the same kind." The thought that devastates us most is that we're alone . . . that nobody understands, or cares. As Christians, however, we never have to fear that. For within us dwells infinite comfort and care in the person of the Holy Spirit.

F. Your life is inseparably linked to Christ Himself.

"After a little while the world will behold Me no more; but you will behold Me; because I live, you shall live

---

3. *Paraklētos* comes from the verb *parakaleō*—"to call to one's side to help." "A *paraklētos* might be a person *called in* to give witness in a law court in someone's favour; he might be an advocate *called in* to plead someone's cause when someone was under a charge which would issue in serious penalty; he might be an expert *called in* to give advice in some difficult situation. He might be a person *called in* when, for example, a company of soldiers were depressed and dispirited to put new courage into their minds and hearts. Always a *paraklētos* is *someone called in to help* when the person who calls him in is in trouble or distress or doubt or bewilderment." William Barclay, *The Gospel of John,* vol. 2, The Daily Study Bible Series (Edinburgh, Scotland: Saint Andrew Press, 1956), p. 194.

also. In that day you shall know that I am in My
Father, and you in Me, and I in you." (vv. 19–20)
The world lives by sight, and when Jesus is out of sight, He's
out of mind. But Christians live by faith (2 Cor. 5:7) and see the
eternal dimension of Christ behind their circumstances. We have
the confidence that whatever circumstances befall us, they can
work together for the good of conforming us to Christ's image
(Rom. 8:28–29).

> ## Training the Eye to See
> Our ability to see is influenced largely by what we have
> been trained to look for. A doctor will see more by looking
> down the throat of a sick child than any parent could. An
> artist will appreciate a tour through a gallery much more
> than someone without those sensibilities. A seamstress will
> appreciate a finely tailored outfit much more than some-
> one whose eyes have not been trained to notice such
> subtleties of style and precision.
> So, too, if our eyes are trained to see God's hand in our
> circumstances, then each pressure indenting the clay of
> our lives will be seen not to bend us out of shape but to
> mold us into vessels of honor—fit for a king.

III. Techniques That Strengthen the Heart
In verses 21–24 we find three principles that will strengthen our
weak hearts.
"He who has My commandments and keeps them, he it is
who loves Me; and he who loves Me shall be loved by My
Father, and I will love him, and will disclose Myself to
him." Judas (not Iscariot) said to Him, "Lord, what then
has happened that You are going to disclose Yourself to
us, and not to the world?" Jesus answered and said to
him, "If anyone loves Me, he will keep My word; and My
Father will love him, and We will come to him, and make
Our abode with him. He who does not love Me does not
keep My words; and the word which you hear is not Mine,
but the Father's who sent Me."
If you look closely at verse 21, you'll notice the words "has . . .
keeps . . . loves." They relate directly to the three realms of worry
that so often trouble our hearts: fear . . . anxiety . . . love. First, knowledge of the truth removes fear. It's remarkable how information
from God's Word takes away the superstition and trauma of death.
Second, application of the knowledge reduces anxiety. Note the

phrase "and keeps them." That means making God's Word a vital part of our lives. Third, love for the Lord releases guilt. Love is the highest of motivations, and when we love the Lord, we desire to please Him (compare 2 Cor. 5:9).

More Tranquil Words

At the beginning of this chapter, Jesus calmed the disciples with words about His Father's house. If that is not enough to still your troubled heart, Jesus spoke more tranquil words at the end of our passage. He said that while you remain on earth in your temporary tent (2 Cor. 5:1), He and the Father will make their home in your heart and dwell in it (John 14:23). Just like the glory of the Lord filled the tabernacle in the wilderness, so the Trinity will fill your heart with their majestic presence. And that light residing in you is sufficient to dispel even the darkest and most foreboding of shadows!

Living Insights

Study One

Fear, anxiety, and guilt ... these three words cripple people every day. But John 14 contains the prescription to remedy these maladies. Let's do more study on the truths that quiet the heart.

- For each of the following six truths, write down cross-references from other portions of the New Testament. You'll see quickly that the truths are not isolated to John's Gospel but are found in a variety of passages throughout the writings of Matthew, Mark, Luke, Paul, and Peter, as well as in John's other books.

Truths That Quiet the Heart

1. Personal faith in a personal God brings personal strength.

_____

_____

2. While preparing a place for us, Christ is preparing us for that place.

_____

_____

Continued on next page

3. The sovereign hand of God is at work.

_____

_____

4. Greater things occur when we pray in Jesus' name, that the Father may be glorified.

_____

_____

5. You are not alone; you have an inward Helper.

_____

_____

6. Your life is inseparably linked to Christ Himself.

_____

_____

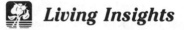 *Living Insights*

Study Two ━━━━━━━━━━━━━━━━━━━━━━━━━━━━━━━━

How do you deal with fear, anxiety, and guilt? There are a variety of effective methods, but none are more helpful than prayer. Paul said it well: "Be anxious for nothing, but in everything by prayer and supplication with thanksgiving let your requests be made known to God" (Phil. 4:6).

• We have learned so many truths to quiet our hearts. Let's pause to give God thanks for the specific seas He has calmed for us in these studies. When you're finished, take some time to pray for yourself, specifically relating to the truths we've been discussing. Close by asking God for strength to achieve victory over fear, anxiety, and guilt.

Overcoming Fear
John 14:25–31

Earlier in his Gospel, John recounted a dramatic story of overcoming fear (6:16–21).

The disciples had piled into a boat to row across the Sea of Galilee. A calm settled over the waters that moonless evening—a calm that was shattered by the force of an incoming storm. Like a woman in the throes of childbirth, the sea swelled with undulating momentum. And with every contraction, their small boat yawed in helpless response.

Stinging rain pelted the disciples, and the boat was taking on water . . . fast. Drenched to the bone, the disciples bailed and rowed even more furiously. But blinded by merciless whips of seawater, they realized the utter futility of their desperate efforts. And within, their fears raged in velocity equal to that of the wind and waves around them.

Then the disciples looked up—Jesus was walking toward them. "It is I," He said. "Do not be afraid." And that's all it took to alleviate their fears. Suddenly the storm was over, and they found themselves safely on shore.

In our study today, fear is the focal point. Like the Sea of Galilee's thrashing waves, fear loomed over the disciples on the night before Jesus' death. It surrounded them. Overwhelmed them. But just as Jesus had quieted their fears and calmed the storm with His presence, so He promised the presence of another who would do the same when He was gone.

I. When Did Fear Originate?
Fear is an instinct literally as old as Adam.

A. The first appearance of fear. The creeping vine of fear entered Eden through the gates of the Fall. When Adam and Eve disobeyed God and ate the forbidden fruit, fear entwined itself around their hearts.

> When the woman saw that the tree was good for food, and that it was a delight to the eyes, and that the tree was desirable to make one wise, she took from its fruit and ate; and she gave also to her husband with her, and he ate. Then the eyes of both of them were opened, and they knew that they were naked; and they sewed fig leaves together and made themselves loin coverings. And they heard the sound of the Lord God walking in the garden in the cool of the day, and the man and his wife hid themselves from the presence of the Lord God among the trees of the garden. Then the Lord God called to the man,

and said to him, "Where are you?" And he said, "I heard the sound of Thee in the garden, and I was afraid because I was naked; so I hid myself." (Gen. 3:6–10)

B. **The first result of fear.** When Adam and Eve sinned, they suddenly became self-conscious, covering themselves with fig leaves. Like veneer covers particle board with a coat of acceptability, the fig leaves served to hide their splintered relationship with God. Cover-ups began with the Fall and have been used to hide guilt ever since.

II. Why Did Fear Occur?

Upon hearing of Christ's imminent death and their inability to go with Him (John 13:33), the disciples found themselves in a swirling vortex of confusion (14:5, 22). But just as they were about to go under, Jesus threw them a lifeline: "Let not your heart be troubled, nor let it be fearful" (v. 27b). Jesus' words are important—they imply that the disciples had the ability to control the reactions of their hearts. And if they could keep their emotions afloat during the tempests *they* experienced, maybe there's hope for *us* as well.

III. How Is Fear Overcome?

In verses 25–31, we find four distinct means of power to abate fear's consuming undertow.

A. **Depending on the person of the Holy Spirit.** Verses 25–26 reveal that the Holy Spirit will buoy us up in Christ's absence.

"These things I have spoken to you, while abiding with you. But the Helper, the Holy Spirit, whom the Father will send in My name, He will teach you all things, and bring to your remembrance all that I said to you."

Underscore the word *all* in verse 26: "all things . . . all that I said." Teaching and reminding are two of the Holy Spirit's ministries, as 1 Corinthians 2:10–12 notes.

For to us God revealed them through the Spirit; for the Spirit searches all things, even the depths of God. For who among men knows the thoughts of a man except the spirit of the man, which is in him? Even so the thoughts of God no one knows except the Spirit of God. Now we have received, not the spirit of the world, but the Spirit who is from God, that we might know the things freely given to us by God.

How does this relate to fear, you may ask. Well, we are usually overcome by fear because we either *ignore* what God has said or *forget* what He has said. And the Holy Spirit's ministry bridges that important information gap, giving us insight and recall. John reiterates this in his first epistle.

And as for you, the anointing which you received from Him abides in you, and you have no need for anyone to teach you; but as His anointing teaches you about all things, and is true and is not a lie, and just as it has taught you, you abide in Him. (1 John 2:27)

B. Claiming the peace of Jesus Christ. In John 14:27, Jesus promises the disciples peace to calm their troubled hearts.

"Peace I leave with you; My peace I give to you; not as the world gives, do I give to you. Let not your heart be troubled, nor let it be fearful."

But the peace Christ promises is not the power of positive thinking. It is not feelings the disciples have to conjure up or circumstances they have to cover up. It is a legacy: "Peace I leave *with* you" (emphasis added). And it is a treasure: "My peace I give *to* you" (emphasis added). His definition of peace is not the same as the world's—tranquil circumstances. Rather, it is an inner calm in the midst of tempestuous outer storms.

"These things I have spoken to you, that in Me you may have peace. In the world you have tribulation, but take courage; I have overcome the world." (16:33)

This type of peace is foreign to the wicked, in whose souls rage a hurricane of heartache.

But the wicked are like the tossing sea,
For it cannot be quiet,
And its waters toss up refuse and mud.
"There is no peace," says my God, "for the wicked."
(Isa. 57:20–21)

C. Accepting the plan of the future. Jesus had informed the disciples of His planned departure (John 13:33, 14:2–3), but they had trouble accepting it. Verses 28–29 of chapter 14 tell why.

"You heard that I said to you, 'I go away, and I will come to you.' If you loved Me, you would have rejoiced, because I go to the Father; for the Father is greater than I. And now I have told you before it comes to pass, that when it comes to pass, you may believe."

Why did the disciples choke on this revelation? Because their love for Jesus was deficient. Sure, they loved Him . . . but not as they should. Theirs was a selfish affection, a desire to keep rather than share.

Averting an Emotional Tug-of-War

Although God has given us people and things to enjoy, it's important to hold them with a loose grasp. Someday,

God may choose to take them from your hands, and the loss will be less painful if you're not clutching them so tightly. What are you clinging to? A job . . . a person . . . your family . . . material possessions . . . the past?

Always remember, the Lord not only gives but He may someday take away that which He has, for a time, entrusted to your care (see Job 1:20–22). And if He does, your possessiveness could find you in a tug-of-war with God.

D. Following the pattern of obedience. Even facing death and Satan himself, Jesus exudes a calm that sets an example for the disciples, and for us.

> "I will not speak much more with you, for the ruler
> of the world is coming, and he has nothing in Me;
> but that the world may know that I love the Father,
> and as the Father gave Me commandment, even so I
> do. Arise, let us go from here." (John 14:30–31)

In verse 28, the *deficiency* of the disciples' love for Christ was highlighted. But now, in verse 31, it is the *sufficiency* of Christ's love for the Father that is in sharp relief. Obedience, motivated by love, gives Jesus a warm blanket of peace in the midst of the chilling storm front beginning to roll into His life. And His obedience sets the perfect pattern for us when we find ourselves left alone in a torrential downpour of fateful circumstances.

When the Waves Get Rough

Though the wind and waves obey Him, Christ may not calm all the outer storms in your life. But He can take your fearful heart and transform it into a calm, inner eye of faith in the midst of those storms. First, however, you must learn to trust Him.

> "The steadfast of mind Thou wilt keep in perfect
> peace,
> Because he trusts in Thee." (Isa. 26:3)

If you're floundering in this area, here are some practical suggestions that will help anchor you. One, acknowledge Jesus Christ as your source of power. Two, begin your day with prayer and claim His peace. Three, correct any habits of pessimism by mooring yourself to His prophetic Word. Four, devote yourself to obedience.

As the Prince of Peace, Jesus merits not only your trust but your obedience as well—even when those waves get rough.

🌳 *Living Insights*

Having come from John 6, the pinnacle of Christ's popularity on earth, to John 14, the beginning of His last days of earthly ministry, we bring our study guide to a close. Let's wrap up our study with a review.

● The following exercise will help you recall what you've learned and apply it to your life. Flip back through the pages of your study guide and Bible. As you retrace your steps, look for one special truth and one important application from each of the lessons. Then write your findings in the space provided.

FOLLOWING CHRIST . . . THE MAN OF GOD

God's Specialty: Impossibilities

Truth: _____

Application: _____

_____

Bread Delivered from Heaven

Truth: _____

Application: _____

_____

Jesus in the Lions' Den

Truth: _____

Application: _____

_____

Letters in the Sand

Truth: _____

Application: _____

_____

Reasons for Rejection

Truth: _____

Continued on next page

Study One—Continued

Application: _____

_____

Blind Men's Bluff

Truth: _____

Application: _____

_____

The Living Door

Truth: _____

Application: _____

_____

Back from Beyond

Truth: _____

Application: _____

_____

Seeking before Hiding

Truth: _____

Application: _____

_____

Humility Personified

Truth: _____

Application: _____

_____

How High Is Your A.Q.?

Truth: _____

Application: _____

_____

Agapē . . . Authentic Love

Truth: _____

Application: _____

_____

Tranquil Words for Troubled Hearts

Truth: _____

Application: _____

_____

Overcoming Fear

Truth: _____

Application: _____

_____

 *Living Insights*

Study Two ━━━━━━━━━━━━━━━━━━━━━━━━━━━━━━━

As a final exercise to close this study guide, look over John 6–14 one more time, and take special note of major events in Christ's life. In each case, look carefully at how Jesus responds to situations and problems that come up.

● Determine specific aspects of Christ's character, seen in His responses to these situations, that you can imitate. Watch how He avoids further discord by choosing not to respond in ways that would normally be expected from you or me and mark the differences. As you review, write your observations below. Pray that God would enable you to live more like Christ, following Him as your model—the Man of God.

Observations of Christ's Character

_____

_____

_____

Continued on next page

Study Two—Continued

_____

_____

_____

_____

_____

_____

_____

_____

_____

_____

_____

_____

_____

_____

_____

_____

_____

Books for Probing Further

"I am the good shepherd; the good shepherd lays down His life for the sheep" (John 10:11).

Jesus is the Good Shepherd.
His sheep shall not want.
He maketh the five thousand lie down in green pastures
    and feedeth them.
He leadeth His disciples beside the still waters of humility
    and washeth their feet.
He restoreth love to the soul of an adulterous woman,
        light to the eyes of a man born blind,
        life to a dead Lazarus.
With rod and staff He watches over His sheep,
        protecting them,
        assuring them,
        comforting them.
Until at last, the pharisaical wolves
        pack together,
        close in,
        and corner the Good Shepherd.
But in the face of sharp, angry teeth,
        bared for the kill,
        He stands His ground.
And with crimson love,
Lays down His life
For the sheep.

—Ken Gire

As the Good Shepherd, Jesus not only died for His sheep, He lived for them as well, nourishing them with His teaching and healing their wounds with His love. To further nourish you in your study of the Gospel of John, we recommend the following books that tie in to the subjects we've covered.

Coleman, Robert E. *The Master Plan of Discipleship.* Old Tappan, N.J.: Fleming H. Revell Co., 1987. The author—director of the School of World Mission and Evangelism at Trinity Evangelical Divinity School— examines the book of Acts to set forth principles of church growth through evangelism and discipleship. He reveals that while specific procedures of evangelism and discipleship change over the years, the basic pattern of the Great Commission has remained unchanged since it was originally given.

Crabb, Lawrence J., Jr., and Dan B. Allender. *Encouragement: The Key to Caring.* Grand Rapids, Mich.: Zondervan Publishing House, 1984.

This book is written for lay people who want to heighten their awareness of other people's problems and want to counsel others with encouragement. The authors show how to penetrate superficial relationships to meet the emotional needs of others, how to avoid the pitfalls of manipulation and of sharing without discretion, and how to counsel with a well-timed word.

France, R. T. *The Evidence for Jesus.* Downers Grove, Ill.: InterVarsity Press, 1986. The author explores the issues surrounding the historicity of Christ, examining in detail a whole range of data. From archaeological evidence and other non-Christian sources to Christian writing both inside and outside the New Testament, France convincingly defends the reliability of the biblical text and the reality of a historical Jesus. This book is a valuable resource to anyone with hard questions about the person of Christ.

Griffiths, Michael. *The Example of Jesus.* Downers Grove, Ill.: InterVarsity Press, 1985. People were drawn to Jesus by His warmth, compassion, and commitment. Later, Paul urged others to follow him as he followed the example of Christ. People today are still drawn to Him, wanting to emulate His example. But how do we become like Jesus? How do we become gloriously conformed to His image as opposed to simply putting on a religious mask? In this thorough study, Griffiths holds the Savior up to the light and allows us to see His radiant, multicolored splendor, motivating us from within to be like Him.

Hadidian, Allen. *Discipleship.* Chicago, Ill.: Moody Press, 1987. A practical, step-by-step guide to discipling, this book is full of material to help answer your questions on the subject and equip you to begin effectively building Christ into the lives of others.

Jacks, Bob and Betty, with Ron Wormser, Sr. *Your Home, a Lighthouse.* Colorado Springs, Colo.: NavPress, 1986. Here's a practical guidebook that grew out of the authors' years of experience with evangelistic Bible studies. You'll learn how to start a study at your home, office, or campus. You'll find out who to invite, what to study, how to ask good questions, and how to answer them . . . and when to encourage a decision for Christ. This helpful book even includes an effective, ready-to-use, evangelistic Bible study on the Gospel of John. Ultimately, however, you'll discover that the secret to introducing others to Jesus isn't in your personal skills or your persuasiveness with people. It's in a simple love for the Lord, a heartfelt concern for the non-Christian, and the power of God's Spirit and of His Word.

Peterson, Jim. *Evangelism for Our Generation.* Colorado Springs, Colo.: NavPress, 1985. This book will help you relax in living out your faith by equipping you with practical principles for developing a relation-ship, modeling the Christian message, and presenting the claims of Christ. Peterson also includes a step-by-step investigative study of the Gospel of John, an important tool that can help a friend or group answer the questions: Who is Jesus, and what does He want of me?

Acknowledgments

Insight for Living is grateful for kind permission to quote from the following sources:

Barclay, William. *The Gospel of John.* Vol. 1. Revised edition. The Daily Study Bible Series. Edinburgh, Scotland: Saint Andrew Press, 1975.

————. *The Gospel of John.* Vol. 2. The Daily Study Bible Series. Edinburgh, Scotland: Saint Andrew Press, 1956.

Notes

Notes